PERPETUAL PEACE

and other essays

Immanuel Kant

PERPETUAL PEACE

and other essays

on POLITICS, HISTORY, and MORALS

Translated, with Introduction,
by TED HUMPHREY

HACKETT PUBLISHING COMPANY
Indianapolis / Cambridge

Immanuel Kant
1724–1804

23 22 21 20   10 11 12 13

Cover design by Richard L. Listenberger
Interior design by James N. Rogers

For further information, please address
    Hackett Publishing Company, Inc.
    P.O. Box 44937
    Indianapolis, IN 46244-0937

    www.hackettpublishing.com

Library of Congress Cataloging-in-Publication Data

Kant, Immanuel, 1724–1804.
    Perpetual peace, and other essays on politics, history,
and moral practice.
    (HPC philosophical classics series)
    Bibliography: p.
    Includes index.
    1. History—Philosophy—Addresses, essays, lectures.
2. Political science—Addresses, essays, lectures.
3. Ethics—Addresses, essays, lectures. 4. Future life—
Addresses, essays, lectures. I. Humphrey, Ted,
1941–   . II. Title. III. Series.
B2758   1982   193   82-11748
ISBN 0-915145-48-0
ISBN 0-915145-47-2 (pbk.)

ISBN-13: 978-0-915145-48-5 (cloth)
ISBN-13: 978-0-915145-47-8 (pbk.)

In Memoriam
Herbert Marcuse
Critical Mind; Enlightened Spirit

Contents

Translator's Introduction

The essays making up this volume are products of Immanuel Kant's mature philosophical reflection, having been written and published between 1784 and 1795, the period during which his three Critical masterpieces—the *Critique of Pure Reason,* the *Critique of Practical Reason,* and the *Critique of Judgment*—appeared. Although the essays deal with important topics, they may nonetheless be regarded as "incidental" essays, for none of them lays what can reasonably be called foundations for Kant's system of thought. And yet all reflect important aspects of that system, taking up topics that genuinely concern Kant, his time, and all reflective persons—topics to which every fully developed philosophical system must be able to contribute. These include the nature of history and the prospect of historical development; the foundations of political association; the relation between principles of morality and those of prudence and happiness; and finally, the nature and prospect of an afterlife. Understandably, Kant is never less than serious here; his reasoning is precise, his vocabulary consistent from essay to essay and from topic to topic, and his voice earnest, often quite fervent.

In a way not readily apparent in the main body of the Critical philosophy, one can see in these essays that Kant is, as a matter of fact, an Enlightenment thinker, for the issues he discusses are those that tended to absorb his Enlightenment predecessors most. For many reasons, we often overlook Kant's relation to the Enlightenment: First, he flourished toward the end of the Enlightenment period, whose dates are normally set at 1689 to 1789. Second, the three *Critiques* address traditional philosophical problems in such an innovative, pristine, and austere way that it is difficult for us to identify them with Enlightenment concerns as such. Third, the writings that most clearly show him to be a product of the Enlightenment were either produced early in his career—before 1770—or are simply overshadowed by the Critical tomes. Futhermore, Kant stands outside the main thrust of Enlightenment thinking, rejecting the view inherited from Descartes and Locke and almost universally held by Enlightenment thinkers: that the key to and core of mankind's advancement is increase of knowledge. Where other Enlightenment figures such as Locke, Voltaire, and D'Alembert argued that increase of knowledge would, on the one hand, provide fuel for driving the machine of man's technological mastery of the environment, thereby improving the material conditions of his life—and, on the other, reduce superstition and intolerance by casting religious and moral differences in a clearer light, thus freeing society of destructive fanaticisms—Kant saw increase of knowledge in and of itself to have no such beneficial effects. Though belief that knowledge is intrinsically empowering and salvific is something of a philosophical credo—one originating with and most convincingly argued by Plato—Kant regards knowledge as no more than a means to an end: Unless knowledge can be put in the service of appropriate ends, it cannot truly benefit individuals or society. For Kant, then, such enlightenment as derives from mere scientifically applicable knowledge is subordinate to enlightenment of a moral nature.

The concern common to all these essays is moral enlightenment, a concern that provides Kant's writing on history, politics, and religion with its guiding thread. Kant's summary view of enlightenment is found in the opening paragraph of his short essay, *An Answer to the Question: What is Enlightenment?*

> *Enlightenment is man's emergence from his self-imposed immaturity. Immaturity* is the inability to use one's understanding without guidance from another. This immaturity is *self-imposed* when its cause lies not in lack of understanding, but in lack of resolve and courage to use it without guidance from another. *Sapere Aude!* "Have courage to use your own understanding!"—that is the motto of enlightenment. (35)[1]

In this essay Kant never makes clear the specific nature of the intellectual immaturity that concerns him, but we can identify two aspects of it: First, Kant had, in the *Critique of Pure Reason,* isolated and attempted to find a solution for epistemological and metaphysical immaturity, by virtue of which, in adopting either traditional rationalism or traditional empiricism, persons allow their thinking to be slavishly guided either by innate ideas or by sense awareness. Thus, one way to read Kant's admonition that we ought to give up our old patterns of thought and see if we might fare better by adopting a new pattern—a way for which the motto is "reason has insight only into that which it produces after a plan of its own, and . . . it must not allow itself to be kept, as it were, in nature's leadingstrings. . . ." (B xiii)—is as a call to enlightenment. Second, in the moral sphere, including politics and religion, thinkers of the period tended to adopt views that appealed either to authority, e.g., God, or to man's natural desires. On both sets of issues and in contrast to both competing traditions, Kant identifies reason (and will) as the focal point of an autonomy enjoyed by man and other free rational beings; and autonomy is just the ability to be self-guiding.[2] This concept is the key to and core of Kant's concept of enlightenment.

As I shall make clear, enlightenment, for Kant, takes place in two stages: the first, propaedeutic to the second, occurs in overthrowing the intellectual bondage inherent in rationalism and empiricism; the second begins with realizing that persons may justifiably believe that they are free rational creatures and actually progresses in the course of their moral growth. This latter notion most accurately captures Kant's sense of enlightenment. How Kant conceives of such moral growth and how he believes it comes about are the focal themes of what follows.[3]

Kant's Overthrow of Dogmatism. Writers can be extraordinarily misleading when offering clues about the original inspiration for or ultimate goals of their work. On the surface Kant seems no more helpful than most, for he provides not just one such clue, but three that do not seem immediately compatible. The most prominently placed clue is in the Preface to the second edition of the *Critique of Pure Reason:*

> I have therefore found it necessary to deny *knowledge* [*Wissen*], in order to make room for *faith* [*Glaube*]. The dogmatism of metaphysics, that is, the preconception that it is possible to make headway in metaphysics without a previous criticism of pure reason, is the source of all that unbelief [*Unglaube*], always very dogmatic, which wars against morality. . . .
> . . . Criticism alone can sever the root of *materialism, fatalism, atheism, free-thinking, fanaticism,* and *superstition,* which can be *injurious universally; as well as idealism* and *scepticism,* which are dangerous chiefly to the Schools, and hardly allow of being handed on to the public.[4]

Kant's claim that he has to "deny knowledge in order to make room for faith" because "dogmatism in metaphysics" is "the source of all that unbelief . . . which wars against morality" actually incorporates his two statements concerning the stimuli that set him on the path toward the criticism of reason and the critical system of philosophy itself. We may conceive the progression as follows: Kant was from the outset concerned to justify his view that mankind is morally responsible for its actions. To be so, persons must be free and rational; and we can assume from passages late in the *Critique of Pure Reason* (passages to be discussed later) that Kant had an unshakable belief, based on direct self-awareness, that man is free and rational. However, this belief could not, in Kant's view, be justified within the context of the fundamental metaphysical attitudes of his time, because these latter held that the crucial metaphysical concepts—of, for example, causality, substance, and possibility and necessity—were true of reality as such. These attitudes he characterizes as "the dogmatism of metaphysics," in the passage quoted above. Moreover, Kant regarded all his important predecessors—whether they were rationalists such as Descartes, for example, who argues that the fundamental concepts of metaphysics are innate, or empiricists such as Locke and Berkeley, who argue that we learn them only through our experiential encounters with the world—as dogmatists; for no matter what their differences, both groups insisted that these concepts apply directly to aspects of beings and the relations among them included in reality as such. The pernicious result of this dogmatism of metaphysics, as Kant sees it, is that it leads to what he calls the antinomy of reason with itself. An antinomy consists of two equally well argued positions—conceived in the same fundamental terms and concerned with the same issue—between which it is impossible to make a rational decision.

As Kant must have conceived the situation early in his career, and as he sets it up in the *Critique of Pure Reason,* the antinomy concerning freedom is as follows: "*Thesis* Causality in accordance with laws of nature is not the only causality from which the appearances of the world can one and all be derived. To explain these appearances it is necessary to assume that there is also another causality, that of freedom." (A 444/B 472) "*Antithesis* There is no freedom; everything in the world takes place solely in accordance with laws of nature." (A 445/B 473) Both rationalists and empiricists could and did consistently adopt either side of the antinomy. The problem was that no counter-arguments against either side were adequate to overthrow them, and the issue as to the existence of freedom—perhaps the most important issue which humans have to decide—was rationally indeterminate. Hence, the issue as to whether or not man is morally responsible is left hanging—and the rational person, lacking justification for any view he may want to hold in relation to it, is driven to skepticism, lack of belief in and lack of commitment to either side. Skepticism undermines morality as a rationally adopted point of view.

This we may assume was Kant's unhappy state when David Hume interrupted his dogmatic slumber. Kant's own statement about what he learned from Hume is in the *Prolegomena:*

> . . . he inferred that reason was altogether deluded with reference to this concept [causality], which she erroneously considered as one of her children, whereas in reality it was nothing but a bastard of imagination, impregnated by experience, which subsumed certain representations under the law of association, and mistook a subjective necessity (custom) for an objective necessity arising from insight. Hence he inferred that reason had no power to think such connections, even in general, because the concepts would then be purely fictitious and all her pretended a priori cognitions nothing but common experiences marked with a false stamp. This is as much as to say that there is not, and cannot be, any such thing as metaphysics at all. (*Prolegomena,* 258)

The salutary effect of Hume's analysis of causality for Kant was that it did, indeed, jolt him from time-worn and unfruitful ways of thinking; but Hume's own views, as Kant saw them, had two completely unacceptable results. First, they deny a priori status—i.e., the property of being logically prior to and independent of sense awareness—to metaphysical concepts; and second, they deny the possibility of metaphysics as a rational undertaking. Hume, too, is a skeptic. But Kant may have received yet another clue from Hume, one that led directly to his own views about the nature and scope of human knowledge and about the possibility of metaphysics. Hume's "destructive metaphysics," as Kant called it, consists of resolving some of the most important metaphysical concepts—causality, object, and self, for instance—into associations of sense impressions and ideas and of identifying these associations as the ways in

which the human mind comes by habit to fill the gaps among and otherwise interpret the actual impressions and ideas of which we are directly
aware. In other words, Hume regarded the essential content and reference of the metaphysical concepts to be the relations among those groups
of impressions and ideas that, for example, we identify as objects or as
causally related.[5] Kant comes to such a view as well, although he turns
the tables on Hume as far as the a priori status of metaphysical concepts
is concerned. Kant found unacceptable not only Hume's destruction of
metaphysics, but also his skepticism, which denied a place to a rationally
based morality. Hence, Kant had to pursue his own course in denying
knowledge so as to make room for morality. We now turn onto the path
he follows.

   Kant's strategy for limiting the pretensions of knowledge began with
some reflections on the nature of space that he published in 1768 under
the title *Concerning the Ultimate Foundation of the Differentiation of
Regions in Space.*[6] In this essay he commented on an aspect of the spatial
organization of objects in the world as we experience it that could not be
accounted for by one of the theories then most current: Leibniz's. That
aspect Kant referred to as incongruent counterparts, the property by virtue of which, for example, left and right hands cannot be superimposed
on one another, even though they comprise the same parts and all the
local spatial relations among those parts are the same. This being so,
space could not, as Leibniz contended, be made up solely as a function of
the relations among existing objects and their parts. Nor could Kant accept Newton's view that space pre-exists all other physical entities, serving as their container, so to speak. This view, according to Kant, makes
of space a mysterious "infinite, self-subsistent non-thing." (A 39/B 56)
By 1770, when he published his Inaugural Dissertation, *On the Form and
Principles of the Sensible and Intelligible World,* Kant had formulated a
revolutionary theory of space and time that became the basis for his
critical system of philosophy.[7] As the view originally set forth in 1770
came finally to be expressed in the *Critique of Pure Reason,* it attributes
four fundamental properties to space and time. Space and time are a
priori, necessary, sensuous, and present to consciousness as infinite.
That is to say, space and time are logically prior to and independent of
specific acts of sense awareness. Moreover, we cannot be conscious of
anything except insofar as it is spatio-temporally organized, although in-
trospective self-awareness and thought have only temporal organization.
Space and time come before consciousness presentationally, not conceptually; or, as Kant says, they contain objects within themselves, and objects are not subsumed under them. Finally, the space and time of which
we are thus aware are intrinsically without limits.[8] Kant argues that this
peculiar combination of properties requires that the space and time of
which humans are directly and immediately aware have their origin
within man's capacities for experiencing the world, rather than being
derived from that experience. In other words, his theory holds that
humanly intuited space and time are not properties of reality as such—of
things as they are in themselves—but are instead matrices of relations ac-

cording to which the objects of human awareness are organized by our cognitive faculties. Kant described this new theory of space and time by saying that the two are transcendentally ideal but empirically real.[9] By this he means, on the one hand, that space and time have their origin in human sensibility—while on the other, that everything of which we are actually aware, whether it be ourselves or things whose existence is independent of ours, is organized so as to display spatial or temporal properties as we become aware of them.

By itself, this new theory of space and time is sufficient to limit the pretensions of our knowledge claims. For if everything of which we are directly and immediately aware has spatial or temporal properties—a claim no one is much inclined to dispute—and if the source of such properties lies in our own cognitive abilities, then we cannot claim that our sense awareness of things represents them as they are in themselves. Thus, even though we may all share the same kind of spatio-temporally organized perceptual image of reality and are thereby able to communicate among ourselves about what we perceive reality to be, we nonetheless cannot claim that our communally shared awareness of the world actually reveals to us reality as such.

Despite the revolutionary character of Kant's theory of space and time, and despite the unique nature of the argument limiting the scope of human knowledge that Kant based on the theory, he had thus far finished only part of his argument against the dogmatic tradition of metaphysics. Against its empirical branch the argument is fairly devastating inasmuch as for empiricists, all human knowledge properly so-called includes a spatio-temporal aspect. However, rationalists had always held those aspects of human knowledge based on and deriving from sense experience to be suspect and are thus relatively untouched by this argument of Kant's, holding as they did that all knowledge truly worthy of the name is conceptual. In fact, Kant's theory had so far not only failed to overthrow the rationalist's views, but was in essential accord with them, since he agreed with that part of rationalism that holds concepts to be an essential component of all human knowledge. It was thus necessary for him to mount an attack on a second front.

Kant's attack on the rationalist's theory of conceptual knowledge also has its source in writings published early in his career. In 1763 he published an essay entitled *Enquiry Concerning the Clarity of the Principles of Natural Theology and Ethics,*[10] wherein he isolates an important characteristic of mathematical knowledge, one not shared by metaphysical and moral claims. Specifically, all mathematical concepts can, he claims, be constructed in space and time; that is, whenever we want to determine whether or not a mathematical concept is true of things in the world, we set about constructing examples in accord with the concept's meaning or content. The constructed examples provide assurance that the concept actually refers to something sensible and thus has real, as opposed to merely nominal, meaning. By contrast, Kant argues that we never use this process of example construction when attempting to define or otherwise demonstrate the meaningfulness of such metaphysically central concepts as soul, causality, substance, and so on. At most, we attempt to show that our definitions of these concepts are not logically self-contradictory, which, again according to Kant, is only the necessary condition for their meaningfulness, and not a sufficient one, as traditional rationalists claimed. Thus, we generally proceed on the basis of verbal definitions, never returning to some bench mark as an accepted criterion of real meaningfulness.[11] At this point, in 1763, Kant dropped his discussion of the difference between mathematical and metaphysical concepts, and did not return to it until almost ten years later. It then became an issue of great concern to him, a concern that dominated his thinking throughout the 1770s, the "silent decade," which produced the *Critique of Pure Reason,* published in 1781.

In the *Critique* Kant mounts a two-pronged attack on traditional rationalism's theory of concepts and conceptual knowledge. First, he distinguishes between two ways in which the concepts crucial to metaphysical speculation are commonly used. In some instances they are used in relation to actual or possible experience—as, for instance, when we assert that frogs cause warts—a use we shall call cognitive. Here our assertion refers to an experientially confirmable or disconfirmable event in the context of which we attach a specific meaning to the concept of causality; namely, that if one handles or otherwise comes into contact with frogs, one will turn up with warts. Here the concept of causality specifies a relation of necessary succession in time between frog handling and wart sprouting. Kant contends that this relation of necessity in and through time makes up the concept of causality's primary and essential reference and content. He provides similar accounts for the other concepts crucial to metaphysics. By contrast to this use of the concept of causality—one that involves an essential reference to some at least possible sensuous or perceptual content—we also find it and similar concepts used in reference to matters of which we are incapable of having any possible experience, as, for example, when we say that God created the world, in contrast to saying that the world has always existed. These statements make assertions about matters that creatures such as ourselves cannot possibly experience, and these are noncognitive. It is logically impossible for us to observe whether or not the universe was created, for doing so requires that we observe either the moment at which time began or the totality of time; and neither observation can possibly be *in* time, which is a necessary condition for *us* to be able to use our standard criteria for applying the concept of causality, the criteria necessary for using them cognitively. In such cases, Kant argues that the concepts crucial to making traditional metaphysical claims derive their sense from their use in contexts where experience is possible, even as we apply them to contexts beyond possible experience. In so applying them, we are not in a position to determine whether or not our claims are true or false. Here, then, our claims are not so much meaningless as essentially *indeterminate* in truth value. This difference between the two uses of the concepts crucial to metaphysics is in Kant's mind when he writes: "Without sensibility no object would be given to us, without understanding no object would be thought. Thoughts without content are empty, intuitions without concepts are blind. It is, therefore, just as necessary to make our concepts sensible, that is, to add the object to them in intuition, as to make our intuitions intelligible, that is, to bring them under concepts." (A 51/B 75) One can see that in laying down this dictum Kant is attempting to assure that the concepts at the core of our understanding of the world have the characteristic that in the early 1760s he had identified as responsible for the real meaningfulness of mathematical concepts, namely, our ability to construct examples of them in space and time. Kant's claim that this procedure is required to assure meaningfulness in our use of the concepts central to metaphysics places him in direct opposition to traditional rationalism and constitutes one part of his overthrow of their theory of conceptual knowledge.

Kant breaks with his rationalist predecessors in yet another way. Where they assumed that such terms as cause or substance refer to some power or property inherent in reality itself, Kant maintains that these terms refer only to the sphere of intuition or perception, all of which is spatio-temporally organized. Hence they do not apply to reality as it is in itself, but only to our awareness of it. Further, rather than referring to powers or properties within the spatio-temporal matrix of experience, the concepts fundamental to knowledge designate specific *possible temporal relations among our perceptions*. Thus, when we say that frogs cause warts, the term 'cause' denotes *the relation of necessity in time* of wart sprouting following upon frog handling. In providing an analysis for these concepts in terms of the unique temporal relations they refer to and allow us to think of as synthetic unities, Kant achieves two goals: (1) he accounts for how we are able to know some truths regarding our experience a priori; (2) at the same time, the conditions attaching to such claims are so restrictive as to disallow traditional metaphysical claims, which do not and cannot involve the reference to intuitable time relations that our normal use of concepts does. Our synthetic a priori knowledge, then, is limited to possible experience; metaphysical claims, similar though they may at first glance be to those other synthetic a priori assertions, make claims about matters that inherently go beyond the boundaries of possible experience.[12] These latter cannot therefore be confirmed or disconfirmed. In this, then, we find the capstone of Kant's denial of knowledge whereby he is able to make room for faith. A priori synthetic knowledge is possible with respect only to the sphere of what we can experience. When we attempt to use our a priori concepts in relation to concerns that overstep the boundaries of possible experience, we lack the guides and criteria we normally rely on to determine the truth or falsity of our statements. Thus, while we may well understand these purported claims to knowledge, we lack all means whatsoever to judge whether or not they are true.

Kant's New Metaphysics. Kant does not simply leave all metaphysical claims in a state of suspension, however. In fact, he moves rather boldly to assert that we have good reasons, if not ones based on cognitive knowledge as such, to affirm the existence of freedom, at least so far as man himself is concerned:

> Man . . . who knows all the rest of nature solely through the senses, knows himself also through pure apperception; and this, indeed, in acts and inner determinations which he cannot regard as impressions of the senses. He is thus to himself, on the one hand phenomenon, and on the other hand, in respect of certain faculties the action of which cannot be ascribed to the receptivity of sensibility, a purely intelligible object. We entitle these faculties understanding and reason. The latter, in particular, we distinguish in a quite peculiar and especial way from all empirically conditioned powers. For it views its object exclusively in light of ideas, and in accordance with them determines the understanding. . . .
>
> . . . That our reason has causality, or that we at least represent it to ourselves as having causality, is evident from the *imperatives* which in all matters of conduct we impose as rules upon our active powers. '*Ought*' expresses a kind of necessity and of connection with grounds which is found nowhere else in the whole of nature. . . .
>
> This '*ought*' expresses a possible action the ground of which cannot be anything but a mere concept; . . . The action to which the '*ought*' applies must indeed be possible under natural conditions. These conditions, however, do not play any part in determining the will itself, but only in determining the effect and its consequences in the [field of] appearances. . . .
>
> Now, in view of these considerations, let us take our stand and regard it as at least possible for reason to have causality with respect to appearances. (A 546/B 574 - A 549/B 577)

More than any other, this passage may be regarded as the watershed of Kant's own metaphysics. In it he makes a number of crucial moves as a result of which man emerges for him as a creature who not only feels the call of duty but who also actually has a moral purpose, a purpose whose nature, moral growth, the essays in this volume sketch.

Kant's crucial claim in this passage is that to oneself each person has a double aspect, one that falls within the same sphere as all other perceivable objects, whereby one sees oneself to be a spatio-temporal object among others, obeying all of the natural laws to which they are subject. To this extent, one can be said merely to appear to oneself. But from another perspective, self-awareness reveals one as an agent who thinks not only about and merely in response to what one perceives—thus about what is and may in the future be the case—but also about what one ought to do. In this passage, the mere fact that man thinks—which Kant views as an action, hence as self-initiated—is sufficient to provide grounds for believing in human freedom; however, he attaches particular importance to the commands that persons issue to themselves, for these commands, signs of freedom though they may be, entail—if they have any meaning whatsoever, i.e., if they are not logically self-contradictory—that persons be free to abide by them, even if only in intention. The command we express whenever we say to ourselves that we ought to do something is not based so much on any set of perceptual facts about the world or ourselves as on our sense that we are free and rational and that this requires us to act in certain ways and not in others. For persons, then, according to Kant, there is an aspect of life whose exclusive foundation is free rationality—the moral life—and its only goal is to further the interests of free rationality; in turn, the interest of free rationality is to protect and revere this quality in all who possess it, to provide for it the circumstances in which to develop. This is Kant's point when he writes.

> Now I say that man, and in general every rational being, exists as an end in himself and not merely as a means to be arbitrarily used by this or that will. He must in all his actions, whether directed to himself or to other rational beings, always be regarded at the same time as an end. . . . rational beings are called persons inasmuch as their nature already marks them out as ends in themselves. . . . Such an end is one for which there can be substituted no other end to which such beings should serve merely as means, for otherwise nothing at all of absolute value would be found anywhere. . . . The practical imperative will therefore be the following: Act in such a way that you treat humanity, whether in your own person or in the person of another, always at the same time as an end and never simply as a means. (*Grounding*, 428–29)

Furthering this interest is neither abstract nor empty, even though based on ideas and commands, rather than on the press of needs and desires.[13] On the one hand, Kant clearly states that although ideas and commands originate in reason, they pertain to and must be regarded by us as capable of having an effect in the realm of appearances, where we live as embodied persons with needs and desires. Thus, as far as our own happiness is concerned, we may reasonably expect that moral action can help bring it about. And yet we are absolutely not to regard these needs and desires as the motives for moral action. Were we to, the initial claim that morality is founded solely on free rationality would be invalidated. For Kant, the only moral motive is respect for the law itself, that is, respect for the principle from which the command or ought, which is the expression of our duty in a given situation, derives. (*Grounding*, 401n.) Now the ideal of practical reason—that is, the ideal of reason insofar as it formulates moral commands for us—is the highest good. The highest good is that idea of reason in which we envision the actual state in which free rational beings are both totally moral and perfectly happy. (See *Crit. Prac. Reason*, 108–109, 110–111.) This idea is not a mere philosophical figment, but one we actually have and express every time we bemoan the fact that virtuous persons seem not to get their just deserts in this world or that the good die young. And though this often seems so, we do not for that reason believe in our calm and noncynical moments that moral action is either irrational or even inefficacious. Indeed, quite to the contrary, it provides grounds for the further beliefs that we must exist as immortal souls, that there must be an afterlife, and that there must be a God from whom each receives his or her just deserts. These are matters in which, as Kant says, free rational creatures have an interest just because they cannot but regard themselves as beings bound by constraints of morality and purpose.

Moral Growth as Man's Essential Purpose.   Just what our purpose is and thus what the nature of history is are fundamental concerns of the essays before us. What Kant conceives the purpose shared by the free rational beings in this world to be, and thus what his view of the nature of history is, are the particular topics of this volume's essays. Here Kant sketches his view that, properly conceived, history is the process—first governed by nature and providence alone, but later, after mankind became aware of its freedom and rationality, increasingly governed by mankind itself—of growing morally: "This portrayal of mankind's earliest history reveals that its exit from that paradise that reason represents as the first dwelling place of its species was nothing but the transition from the raw state of a merely animal creature to humanity, from the harness of the instincts to the guidance of reason—in a word, from the guardianship of nature to the state of freedom." (115) At history's outset and in the midst of its various intermediate stages, we cannot expect that humans have an explicit, reflective plan for their development, for during most of its course mankind's material state is too primitive to allow him to devote his time and energies to such issues; and subsequently, as conditions have permitted, when humans have been able to think about the course of their lives, they have tended to be consumed with matters of personal self-interest to the virtual exclusion of those pertinent to universal well-being. During the early stages, then, the future of mankind as a whole remains largely in nature's care.

On the basis of the doctrine of teleological thinking and judgment that Kant develops in the *Critique of Judgment,*[14] he argues that mankind must regard its development as one of nature's objectives; as such, mankind is destined to develop all of its natural capacities to the highest degree possible, particularly where these support rationality, mankind's highest capacity, even though this does not occur in the individual but only in the species. (18-19) This last point concerns Kant a great deal, for it arises several times in this volume's essays. He seems to lament deeply the fact that in the course of history the individual is subordinate to the development of the species, while the species might actually be served better if at least some few gifted individuals were to live longer. (117) But this conflict between the requirements of the species and those of individuals derives, according to Kant, from the fact that man is a creature whose nature and destiny are to make the transition from a mere natural creature, one whose needs can be met by instinct alone, to a civilized moral being, one whose needs and goals, because they arise from a reason freed from bondage to the immediate necessities of an animal existence, can be satisfied only through applied reason and free choice. (116f.)

Much in the same way that the limited scarcity hypothesis sets up for Hume the fundamental problem of morality,[15] mankind's transition from merely animal existence to free rational creature is at the center of Kant's conception of the fundamental moral problem. This is precisely the point he makes, though in the most abstract of terms, when he writes in the *Grounding for the Metaphysics of Morals,* "For the will stands, as it were, at a crossroads between its a priori principle, which is formal, and its a posteriori incentive, which is material. . . ." (*Grounding,* 400) Were man merely an animal creature therefore limited to instinctual needs satisfiable by instinctive responses to the world, no problem of a properly moral kind would arise. The specifically human moral problem crops up in part because man has both instinctual needs—food, sex, and shelter, not to mention play and other sorts of physical enjoyment—as well as those deriving from free rationality. In addition, simply because he is free and rational, and because these are for Kant mankind's highest capacities, nature seems to have placed another burden on it, one that Kant characterizes in this way: "*Nature has willed that man, entirely by himself, produce everything that goes beyond the mechanical organization of his animal existence and partake in no other happiness or perfection than what he himself, independently of instinct, can secure through his own reason.*" (19) This remarkable claim makes unequivocally clear Kant's conviction that man's essence is free rationality, not animal nature. Once man breaks with the instincts in meeting his needs, once his needs are transformed into desires, his entire relation to himself, other persons, and the rest of creation is also changed. For now he must not only decide which of his needs to meet first and in what ways and to what degree, but he must also determine how best to meet them within the context of the competition and the conflicts among priorities that he finds himself to have with his fellows. Here all becomes a matter of choice, not, of course, simple personal, but social choice, for without social agreement, be it implicit or explicit, humans will remain embroiled in a Hobbesian state of war. (297f.) In presenting the species with this problem—that of working out for itself the means whereby it is to develop from a mere animal creature to a fully free and rational one—Kant remarks that nature seems to have "aimed more at his rational *self-esteem* than at his well-being," (20) a comment that points out the moral nature of the project.

The human characteristic serving as the means through which humanity's capacities come to be refined is "antagonism," which Kant also calls "unsocial sociability" (*Ungesellige Geselligkeit*). This characteristic permeates all levels of human relations, beginning with those among single individuals and extending to those among nations. All individuals —be they persons, families, peoples, or nations—have needs that they cannot by themselves adequately meet; this forces them to seek out relations with other individuals, even though the competing needs of these same individuals, along with their self-interested desire to get as much for themselves at the expense of others as is possible, drives them into conflict. Despite this conflict, and oftentimes precisely because of it, the original needs do not diminish and may sometimes become even more pressing. This dialectic creates situations in which not just compromise born of expediency, but real accommodation of other parties, is necessary. Such accommodation takes the form of recognizing that all parties involved have rights that accrue to them just because they, like oneself, are ends in themselves, who cannot rightfully be used as means to one's own ends, i.e., takes the form of acknowledging them to be persons.

Just what the actual, specific motives for it may have been Kant nowhere says, but underlying the social contract is at least an implicit recognition that the needs of individuals cannot be met adequately unless rights are explicitly acknowledged and protected. Nonetheless, the primary objective of the social contract is not to insure humanity's physical well-being, but to guarantee its individual and collective rights. This is partly because Kant regards mankind's moral nature as incomparably higher than its physical one, but primarily because while its physical needs probably cannot be wholly reconciled, its moral ones can and must be:

> Uniting many for some (common) end (that they all *have*) is a property of all social contracts; but as an end in itself (that each of them *ought to have*) and, consequently, as an end that is an unconditioned and primary duty with respect to every external relation in general among men, who cannot help but to mutually influence one another, this union is met with only in society, and then only insofar as it finds itself in a civil state, i.e., constitutes a commonwealth. Now in such external relations the end [whose pursuit] is in itself a duty and that is the supreme formal condition . . . of all other external duty is the *right* of men *under public coercive law,* through which each can receive his due and can be made secure from the interference of others. (289)

Uniting in a social contract is simply the first stage in working out humanity's personal and collective destiny. Having once formed a nation, a people has still to work out the implications of the fact that while they are united for a single purpose, that purpose is the moral one of bringing persons to the point where they actually realize that their personal rights are best served and protected when they are so limited, by virtue of their own volition, as not to abridge the rights of others. In this process individual wills come to make up a universal will; and this is just the process of moral growth, bringing oneself to adopt the universal will from the pure motive of respect for the right, and of our duty to the right as free rational beings.

Such growth does not occur only on the level of individuals who are members of duly constituted nation states, of course, but also on the level at which nation states relate to one another. And although Kant believes the single greatest problem humanity faces is forming a just civil

constitution, humanity may be most threatened by the intractibility nations display in their relations among themselves. Working out a solution
for the antagonism manifest at this level may, in fact, be more difficult
than doing so within a particular nation state. The cosmopolitan
state—that state in which nations co-exist under the rule of law—is the
only one in which the rights of individuals can be fully guaranteed; yet
such a state of right among nations requires that they—like individuals
who enter into a social contract—submit to a single authority possessing
a coercive right whereby they can be forced to abide by the rule of law.
However, attempting to bring about such a state raises dangers that do
not occur when peoples become nations. Because they are relatively more
self-sufficient than individuals, nations are even more jealous of their
sovereignty and thus less inclined to submit to independent coercive
authority. But even if that obstacle did not bar the way to cosmopolitanism, Kant is hesitant to advocate bringing such an overarching coercive
power into existence, because there is in the competition among nations a
certain degree of protection from the most overbearing despotism;
whereas if all nations were to become subject to a single effective coercive power, the race might be subjected to a despotism that prohibited all
further growth of freedom and responsibility. (367ff.) Kant provides no
solution for this dilemma, and, of course, it is one we face today.

The essays before us address humankind's present state, one that has
not appreciably changed since they were written—except perhaps in that
the race now possesses the means to annihilate itself—a state that the
reader will find Kant to have analyzed acutely. Although we are now just
beginning to recognize what are the rights of a citizen, a free rational person subject to the universal will of all—we have not yet effectively sanctioned those rights. Humanity's moral growth is abridged at every turn
by restrictions on speech and thought and perhaps even more by the
diversion of society's resources away from those institutions that truly
benefit society and individuals, e.g., education, medicine, and the arts,
as well as technology aimed at relieving the duress of the material conditions of our existence, to constant and ever-increasing armament for
war. (345) Mankind may yet come to the "perverse end" of things,
rather than attain to the highest good. (339) But one value of these
essays, as Kant himself points out, is that they not only heighten our
awareness of humanity's present state in light of what our true nature
and destiny ought to be, but they also sketch a plan whereby it can more
effectively be brought about. (30-31) In that regard they further an end
that Kant claims all persons have and that they cannot be indifferent
to—moral growth. That such growth should occur was the object of
Kant's deepest faith, and the Critical philosophy's ultimate goal is to
clear the way for it.

Arizona State University   TED HUMPHREY
Tempe

Endnotes to Translator's Introduction

1. References to Kant's writings are normally placed in the text between parentheses. When references are to essays included in this volume they include only the number(s) found in the *margins* of this volume, which denote pages in volume 8 of the edition of Kant's works issued by the *Preussischen Akademie der Wissenschaften,* cited fully in the bibliography. Except for the *Critique of Pure Reason,* citations to which include only first (A) and second (B) edition page numbers, citations of Kant's other works include an abbreviated title, listed in the full bibliographical citation of each work, and the *Akademie* edition page number, which all of the translations cited include.

2. See *Grounding,* 412.

3. One of the most insightful and elegant accounts of Kant's battle against his dogmatic predecessors is Lewis White Beck's essay, "Kant's Strategy," in Lewis White Beck, *Essays on Kant and Hume,* (New Haven: Yale University Press, 1978), pp. 3–19.

4. B xxx-xxxv. Another of Kant's clues about the inspiration and goals of his writing is found in the *Prolegomena,* written three years before the foregoing passage. He states, "I openly confess that my remembering David Hume was the very thing which many years ago first interrupted my dogmatic slumber and gave my investigations in the field of speculative philosophy a quite new direction." (*Prolegomena,* 260) Finally, in letter written to Christian Garve in 1798, Kant writes: "It was not the investigation of the existence of God, immortality, and so on, but rather the antinomy of pure reason—'the world has a beginning; it has no beginning, and so on,' right up to the 4th [*sic*]: 'There is freedom in man, versus there is no freedom, only the necessity of nature'—that is what first aroused me from my dogmatic slumber and drove me to the critique of reason itself, in order to resolve the scandal of ostensible contradiction of reason with itself." (*Correspondence,* 252) This final clue is by no means conceptually incompatible with the one in the *Prolegomena,* for although the two have different specific references, both are concerned with the nature, origin, and scope of the concept of causality. Hume's "destructive" analysis of that concept—which Kant, unlike Hume, regarded as only one of a coherent set of concepts crucial to metaphysics that would have to receive the same sort of analysis—may well have been the trip-wire that stimulated Kant to give up his old dogmatic assumptions regarding causality. But inasmuch as causality is the crux of the problem of freedom, the need to redirect his thinking

about it provided Kant with an opportunity to follow a new course leading ultimately to his mature account of the concepts crucial to knowledge and metaphysical speculation.

5. See David Hume, *A Treatise of Human Nature,* 2nd ed., ed. L. A. Selby-Bigge, rev. P. H. Nidditch, (Oxford: The Clarendon Press, 1978), pp. 69–274, *passim.*

6. See *Kant: Selected Pre-Critical Writings,* ed. and trans. G. B. Kerferd and D. E. Walford, (New York: Barnes & Noble, 1968), pp. 36–43.

7. See *Kant: Selected Pre-Critical Writings,* pp. 45–92.

8. See A 22/B 37 – A 41/B 58. My "The Historical and Conceptual Relations between Kant's Metaphysics of Space and Philosophy of Geometry," in *The Journal of the History of Philosophy,* XI, No. 4 (1973), pp. 483–512, is a detailed discussion of these issues.

9. See A 28/B 44 and A 35–36/B 52.

10. See *Kant: Selected Pre-Critical Writings,* pp. 5–35.

11. Lewis White Beck discusses these issues in detail in "Kant's Theory of Definition," *Studies in the Philosophy of Kant,* (Indianapolis: The Bobbs-Merrill Co., Inc., 1965), pp. 61–73.

12. The possibility, nature, and limits of synthetic knowledge a priori among finite rational beings like ourselves is the central topic of Kant's *Critique of Pure Reason,* as he makes clear in the Introduction, A 1/B 1 – A 16/B 30. He characterizes such knowledge as consisting of those statements about reality or our awareness of it that actually extend our knowledge, even though such knowledge is logically independent of actual experience. He asserts that all dogmatic metaphysical claims purport to have this property, as they must if they are to be both informative and about matters of which we can have no direct perceptual awareness. The effect of Kant's argument is to limit such claims to matters of possible experience, thereby stripping traditional metaphysical claims of pretensions to *demonstrable* truth (or falsity).

13. Kant defines the term "idea" as follows: "I understand by idea a necessary concept of reason to which no corresponding object can be given in sense experience. Thus, the pure concepts of reason, now under consideration, are *transcendental ideas.* They are concepts of pure reason, in that they view all knowledge gained in experience as being determined through an absolute totality of conditions. They are not arbitrarily invented; they are imposed by the very nature of reason itself,

and therefore stand in necessary relation to the whole employment of understanding. Finally, they are transcendent and overstep the limits of all experience; no object adequate to the transcendental idea can ever be found." (A 327/B 383 - B 384; cp. *Crit. Prac. Reason,* 155f. and *Crit. Judgement,* §49). For Kant, then, the term "idea" has a specific, technical use, and denotes (a) the representation of a *totality,* e.g., God, the world, the self, or the highest good; (b) a representation that is necessary to reason itself; and (c) some object that can never actually be given in experience. The purported objects of ideas are thus matters of faith, not cognitive knowledge.

14. See *Crit. Judgment,* 181–86, 369–72.

15. David Hume, *Enquiry Concerning the Principles of Morals,* 2nd ed., ed. L. A. Selby-Bigge, (Oxford: The Clarendon Press, 1963), Of Justice, pt. 1, pp. 183–92.

Bibliography

A. WRITINGS BY KANT

1. *In German*

Kant, Immanuel. *Kants gesammelte Schriften,* 28 vols. Berlin and Leipzig: Walter de Gruyter & Co., 1904–.

2. *In English Translation*

_____. *Anthropology from a Pragmatic Point of View,* trans. Mary J. Gregor. the Hague: Martinus Nijhoff, 1974. Cited as *Anth.*

_____. *Critique of Judgment,* trans. Werner S. Pluhar. Indianapolis: Hackett Publishing Co., 1987. Cited as *Crit. Judgment.*

_____. *Critique of Practical Reason,* trans. Lewis White Beck. Indianapolis: The Bobbs-Merrill Co., Inc., 1956. Cited as *Crit. Prac. Reason.*

_____. *Critique of Pure Reason,* trans. Norman Kemp Smith. New York: St. Martin's Press, 1963. Cited by A and B page numbers only.

_____. *Grounding for the Metaphysics of Morals,* trans. James W. Ellington. Indianapolis: Hackett Publishing Company, 1981. Cited as *Grounding.*

_____. *Logic,* trans. Robert S. Hartman and Wolfgang Schwarz. Indianapolis: The Bobbs-Merrill Co., Inc., 1974.

_____. *Metaphysical Elements of Justice* (Part I, *The Metaphysics of Morals*), trans. John Ladd. Indianapolis: The Bobbs-Merrill Co., Inc., 1965. Cited as *Met. Elements of Justice.*

_____. *Metaphysical Principles of Virtue* (Part II, *The Metaphysics of Morals*), trans. James Ellington. Indianapolis: Hackett Publishing Co., 1982. Cited as *Met. Prin. of Virtue.*

_____. *Metaphysical Foundations of Natural Science,* trans. James Ellington. In *Philosophy of Material Nature.* Indianapolis: Hackett Publishing Co., 1985.

_____. *Philosophical Correspondence: 1759–1799,* trans. Arnulf Zweig. Chicago: The University of Chicago Press, 1967. Cited as *Correspondence.*

_____. *Prolegomena to Any Future Metaphysics,* trans. James W. Ellington. Indianapolis: Hackett Publishing Co., 1977. Cited as *Prolegomena.*

_____. *Religion Within the Limits of Pure Reason Alone,* trans. Theodore M. Greene and Hoyt W. Hudson. New York: Harper & Row, Publishers, 1960.

_____. *Selected Pre-Critical Writings,* trans. G. B. Kerferd and D. E. Walford. New York: Barnes & Noble, Inc., 1968.

B. WRITINGS ON KANT

1. *General Books on Kant's Philosophy*

Allison, Henry E. *Kant's Transcendental Idealism: An Interpretation and Defense.* New Haven: Yale University Press, 1983.

Beck, Lewis White. *Early German Philosophy.* Cambridge, Mass.: Harvard University Press, 1969. Chapter XVII.

Cassirer, Ernst. *Kant's Life and Thought,* trans. James Haden. New Haven: Yale University Press, 1981.

Guyer, Paul. *Kant and the Claims of Knowledge.* Cambridge: Cambridge University Press, 1987.

Hoffe, Otfried. *Immanuel Kant,* trans. Marshall Farrier. Albany: State University Press of New York, 1994.

Kitcher, Patricia. *Kant's Transcendental Psychology.* Oxford: Oxford University Press, 1990.

Körner, Stephen, *Kant.* New Haven: Yale University Press, 1982.

Strawson, P. F. *The Bounds of Sense.* London: Methuen & Co. Ltd., 1966.

de Vleeschauwer, Herman-J. *The Development of Kantian Thought,* trans. A. R. C. Duncan. London: Thomas Nelson and Sons, Ltd., 1962.

Walker, Ralph C. S. *Kant.* London: Routledge & Kegan Paul, 1978.

Walsh, W. H. *Kant's Criticism of Metaphysics.* Edinburgh: The University Press, 1975.

2. *Books Concerned with Kant's Philosophy of History, Political Theory, and Philosophy of Religion*

Allison, Henry E. *Kant's Theory of Freedom.* Cambridge: Cambridge University Press, 1990.

Arendt, Hannah. *Lectures on Kant's Political Philosophy,* ed. Ronald Beiner. Chicago: The University of Chicago Press, 1982.

Beck, Lewis White. *A Commentary on Kant's Critique of Practical Reason.* Chicago: University of Chicago Press, 1961.

Cassirer, Ernst. *Rousseau, Kant and Goethe.* New York: Harper & Row, 1963.

Despland, Michel. *Kant on History and Religion,* with a translation of Kant's 'On the Failure of All Attempted Philosophical Theodicies.' Montreal and London: McGill-Queen's University Press, 1973.

England, F. E. *Kant's Conception of God.* New York: Humanities Press, 1968.

Galston, William A. *Kant and the Problem of History.* Chicago: University of Chicago Press, 1975.

McFarland, J. D. *Kant's Concept of Teleology.* Edinburgh: The University Press, 1970.

Marcuse, Herbert. *Reason and Revolution: Hegel and the Rise of Social Theory,* 2nd ed. Boston: Beacon Press, 1960.

_____. *Studies in Critical Philosophy,* trans. Joris de Bres. Boston: Beacon Press, 1972.

Mulholland, L. A. *Kant's System of Rights.* New York: Columbia University Press, 1990.

Murphy, Jeffrie G. *Kant: The Philosophy of Right.* Macon: Mercer University Press, 1994.

Philonenko, A. *Théorie et praxis dans la pensée morale et politique de Kant et de Fichte en 1793*. Paris: Vrin, 1968.

Reboul, Olivier. *Kant et le problème du mal*. Montreal: Presses de l'universite Montréal, 1971.

Riley, Patrick. *Kant's Political Philosophy*. Totowa, N.J.: Rowman and Littlefield, 1983.

Schwartländer, Johannes. *Der Mensch Ist Person: Kants Lehre vom Menschen*. Stuttgart: W. Kohlhammer Verlag, 1968.

Stevens, Rex Patrick. *Kant on Moral Practice*. Macon: Mercer University Press, 1981.

Sullivan, Roger J. *Immanuel Kant's Moral Theory*. Cambridge: Cambridge University Press, 1989.

Williams, Howard. *Kant's Political Philosophy*. New York: St. Martin's Press, 1983.

Wood, Allen W. *Kant's Moral Religion*. Ithaca: Cornell University Press, 1970.

_____. *Kant's Rational Theology*. Ithaca: Cornell University Press, 1978.

Yovel, Yirmiahu. *Kant and the Philosophy of History*. Princeton: Princeton University Press, 1980.

3. *Articles Concerned with Kant's Philsophy of History, Political Theory, and Philosophy of Religion*

Allison, Henry E. "Kant's 'Transcendental Humanism'." *The Monist* 55 (1971).

Auxter, Thomas. "The Unimportance of Kant's Highest Good." *Journal of the History of Ideas* XVII, no. 2 (1979).

Axinn, Sidney. "Kant, Logic, and the Concept of Mankind." *Ethics* XLVIII (1958).

Beck, Lewis White. "Kant on the Right of Revolution." *Essays on Kant and Hume*. New Haven: Yale University Press, 1978.

_____. Editor's Introduction to *Kant on History*. Indianapolis: The Bobbs-Merrill Co., Inc., 1963.

Bourke, John. "Kant's Doctrine of 'Perpetual Peace'." *Philosophy* XVII (1942).

Fackenheim, Emil. "Kant and Radical Evil." University of Toronto Quarterly 23 (1953–54).

_____. "Kant's Concept of History." *Kant-Studien* XLVIII (1957).

Greene, Theodore M. "The Historical Context and Religious Significance of Kant's *Religion*. Kant. *Religion within the Limits of Pure Reason Alone.*" New York: Harper & Row, Publishers, 1960.

Jones, W. T. "Purpose, Nature and the Moral Law." Whitney, G. T. and Bowers, P. F. *The Heritage of Kant.* New York: Russell and Russell, 1962.

Kersting, Wolfgang. "Politics, freedom, and order: Kant's political philosophy." Guyer, Paul. *The Cambridge Companion to Kant.* Cambridge: Cambridge University Press, 1992.

Murphy, Jeffrie G. "Kant on Theory and Practice." Shapiro, Ian and DeCew, Judith Wager. *Theory and Practice.* New York: New York University Press, 1995.

Reiss, Hans. "Editor's Introduction." *Kant's Political Writings.* Cambridge: The University Press, 1971.

_____. "Kant and the Right of Rebellion." *Journal of the History of Ideas* XVII (1956).

Silber, John R. "Kant's Conception of the Highest Good as Immanent and Transcendent." *Philosophical Review* LXVIII (1959).

_____. "The Copernican Revolution in Ethics: The Good Reexamined." *Kant-Studien* LI (1959).

_____. "The Ethical Significance of Kant's *Religion*." Kant. *Religion within the Limits of Pure Reason Alone.* New York: Harper & Row Publishers, 1960.

Schwarz, Wolfgang. "Kant's Philosophy of Law and International Peace." *Philosophy and Phenomenological Research* XXIII (1962).

Walsh, W. H. "Kant's Moral Theology." Proceedings of the British Academy 49. London: Oxford University Press, 1964.

Wood, Allen W. "Rational theology, moral faith, and religion." Guyer, Paul. *The Cambridge Companion to Kant.* Cambridge: Cambridge University Press, 1992.

C. OTHER WORDS CITED

1. *Books*

Hume, David. *A Treatise of Human Nature,* 2nd ed., rev., ed. L. A. Selby-Bigge, rev. P. H. Nidditch. Oxford: The Clarendon Press, 1978.

_____. *An Enquiry Concerning the Principles of Morals,* 2nd ed., ed. L. A. Selby-Bigge. Oxford: The Clarendon Press, 1963.

2. *Articles*

Beck, Lewis White. "Kant's Strategy." *Essays on Kant and Hume.* New Haven: Yale University Press, 1978.

_____. "Kant's Theory of Definition." *Studies in the Philosophy of Kant.* Indianapolis: The Bobbs-Merrill Co., Inc., 1965.

Humphrey, Ted B. "The Historical and Conceptual Relations between Kant's Metaphysics of Space and Philosophy of Geometry." *Journal of the History of Philosophy* XI, no. 4 (1973).

A Note on the Text

The standard reference edition of Immanuel Kant's writings is *Kant's gesammelte Schriften,* hrsg. Königliche Preussische Akademie der Wissenschaften, Walter de Gruyter & Co., Berlin and Leipzig, 1904–. This is the edition I have used in making these translations. All the essays in this volume appear in Band VIII (volume 8) of that edition, and the numbers in the margins of the present pages refer to the page numbers in that volume. Kant's own footnotes are designated by a star * or a dagger †, while the translator's are designated by a number, but not placed in brackets. Although I abided exclusively by the edition cited above for my texts, I did occasionally consult other commonly received German editions, specifically, Cassirer's, Vorländer's, and Weischedel's. All these essays have previously been translated into English, some several times, and I made use of those translations in deciding how to render Kant's words into English. In this regard, I wish to acknowledge the dean of American Kant scholars, Lewis White Beck, as well as Robert E. Anchor, E. B. Ashton, Emil L. Fackenheim, Carl J. Friedrich, and Hans Reiss. Further, I have over the years learned a great deal about putting Kant's German into English from reading the masterful translations of James W. Ellington, Robert Hartman and Wolfgang Schwartz, P. G. Lucas, and Arnulf Zweig. I have attempted to produce translations that stand in the tradition of these and the previously mentioned persons, but, of course, only time and the critics can determine whether I have succeeded.

Principles of Translation: This is the first time this set of essays has been translated into English by a single person, one whose training and interest in them is primarily philosophical. My goals have been to produce a text that is faithful to Kant's original, useful to scholars, and accessible to students and other persons who are not expert in Kant's thought. By itself, this should result in having Kant's prose style and conceptually important vocabulary rendered consistently. Although I have striven for this, I sometimes found it necessary to violate the various rules I set out for myself at the beginning of the project. But I have never done so, particularly when a matter of vocabulary arose, without indicating the German in brackets, which also indicate my interpolations in the text. The precepts governing my work include the following: (1) These translations conform as closely as is possible in modern English to Kant's paragraphing, italicization, and punctuation. Unlike all other translators of these essays, I have not attempted to remake Kant's paragraphs or to shorten his sentences, particularly where so doing would violate the logical flow of his reasoning. The fact is that Kant thought in complex patterns, and he seems to have written in such a way as to display the various elements of his thinking and the relations among them that lead to his conclusions. I do not regard his prose style—maddening as it sometimes is—as the result of lack of skill, insensitivity to the difficulties readers might have with his thought, or arrogance, but rather as the natural product of the effort to express the full content of his thinking. It would be a disservice not to try to preserve the sequence of subordinations one finds in his German, for they contain the logical structure of his thought. (2) Throughout the volume, Kant's technical vocabulary receives a consistent English translation, *except* in two notable instances: (a) *Absicht* I render "intention" in contexts involving rational agents, e.g., man or God, but "objective" where Kant is referring to nature; (b) *Zweck* I have sometimes translated "end," or sometimes "purpose," depending on which provided the most idiomatic English, although in general I favor "end."

Two other terminological matters warrant mention. In some slight contrast with the tradition of English translation, I decided to render *das Recht* (and *das Unrecht*), as well as their adjectival forms, as "right" (and "wrong"), rather than "just" (and "unjust"). This is because even where Kant uses these terms in reference to political theory and legality, their conceptual content derives from the context of morality, where these terms denote a moral property of actions, a property that Kant argues can be isolated by using the Categorical Imperative in formulating the maxims for our actions. Because one of Kant's major contentions throughout these essays, especially in *"Theory and Practice"* and *Perpetual Peace,* is that considerations of rightness and wrongness ought to permeate human action in every sphere, taking precedence over all others, I believed it desirable to use terms that for most of us denote moral properties of acts. *Denkungsart* crops up many times in these essays; more, certainly, than I ever expected when I began the project. In Kant's writing it first occurs in a striking way in the Preface to the second edition of the *Critique of Pure Reason* (B xix), where he uses it in developing his famous Copernican Revolution metaphor. I have concluded, based on tracking down Kant's uses of this term throughout the corpus, that it has a technical meaning for him—as a term of art—and I have thus consistently translated it "way of thinking," meaning by this the fundamental attitude or mentality that a person or culture characteristically brings to a problem or set of circumstances. Finally, I have chosen not to capitalize "nature," "providence," "idea," and other such terms, even where Kant writes of them in such a way as to suggest that they may have objectives or be the means whereby such are brought about, or might otherwise be reified. I believe that Kant capitalizes such terms solely as a function of the German convention of capitalizing all nouns, a convention writers of English gave up in the late eighteenth and early nineteenth centuries. Personifying or otherwise reifying what these terms refer to, the result of capitalizing terms in English, is inconsistent with the views on teleological thinking and judgment that Kant expresses in the *Critique of Judgment*. (3) I have attempted to the degree consistent with idiomatic English to reflect a peculiar and, I suspect, significant feature of Kant's prose; namely, its use of two separate and parallel vocabularies, one deriving from Latin and one that has more properly German roots. This is a feature of English as well, e.g., "depose" and "overthrow," the former being Latin in origin, the latter Old English. In general, the latinate vocabulary in both languages is more abstract and more polite—indeed, bloodless—whereas the Anglo-Saxon and German vocabularies are concrete, earthy, and vibrant. I have not been able consistently to render Kant's latinate vocabulary into latinate English and his more properly German vocabulary into Anglo-Saxon English; like all of his translators, I have tended to lapse into or been forced to use a latinate vocabulary. But where I have succeeded in using an Anglo-Saxon vocabulary for his German one, Kant's prose comes across as more muscular and straightforward than we normally think of it as being. Though much maligned in this regard, Kant actually writes rather well, and this often shows through in these essays. I hope my renderings will allow the reader to see that.

Professor James W. Ellington, a reader for the publisher, commented on the entire text: his work was most helpful, and I deeply appreciate it. Special thanks are due to Mrs. Judith Betz, who helped prepare the index. The errors that remain are, of course, my own.

                                                          T. H.

Idea
for a
Universal History
with a Cosmopolitan Intent*1
(1784)

Whatever concept one may form of *freedom of the will* in a meta- 17
physical context, its *appearances,* human actions, like all other natural
events, are certainly determined [*bestimmt*] in conformity with universal natural laws. History—which concerns itself with providing a nar-
rative of these appearances, regardless of how deeply hidden their
causes may be—allows us to hope that if we examine *the play of the
human will's freedom in the large,* we can discover its course to conform to rules [*regelmässig*] as well as to hope that what strikes us as
complicated and unpredictable in the single individual may in the
history of the entire species[2] be discovered to be the steady progress
and slow development of its original capacities. Since the free wills of
men seem to have so great an influence on marriage, the births conse-
quent to it, and death, it appears that they are not subject to any rule
by which one can in advance determine their number; and yet the annual charts that large countries make of them show that they occur in
conformity with natural laws as invariable as those [governing] the unpredictable weather, whose particular changes we cannot determine in
advance, but which in the large do not fail to support a uniform and
uninterrupted pattern in the growth of plants, in the flow of rivers,
and in other natural events. Individual men and even entire peoples
give little thought to the fact that while each according to his own
ways pursues his own end—often at cross purposes with each other—
they unconsciously proceed toward an unknown natural end, as if
following a guiding thread; and they work to promote an end they
would set little store by, even if they were aware of it.

Since in their endeavors men proceed neither merely instinctually,
like animals, nor yet according to a fixed plan, like rational citizens of
the world, it appears that no systematic [*planmässig*] *history of man*
is possible (as perhaps it might be with bees or beavers).[3] One cannot
resist a certain [feeling of] indignation when one sees men's actions
placed on the great stage of the world and finds that, despite some in- 18
dividuals' seeming wisdom, in the large everything is finally woven
together from folly and childish vanity and often even childish malice

*Among the short notices in the twelfth issue of this year's *Gothaische Gelehrte
Zeitung* is a passage that is without doubt based on my conversation with a scholar who
was passing through; it requires the following clarification, without which it would not
conceivably make sense.

and destructiveness. In the end, one does not know what concept one should have of a species so taken with its own superiority. Here, since the philosopher cannot assume that in the great human drama mankind has a rational *end of its own,* his only point of departure is to try to discover whether there is some *natural objective* in this senseless course of human affairs, from which it may be possible to produce a history of creatures who proceed without a plan of their own but in conformity with some definite plan of nature's. We want to see if we can succeed in finding a guiding thread for such a history, and we will leave it to nature to produce the man who is in a position to write it. In this way she produced a Kepler, who in an unexpected way subjected the eccentric paths of the planets to definite laws, and a Newton, who explained these laws by means of a universal natural cause.

First Thesis

All of a creature's natural capacities are destined to develop completely and in conformity with their end. This is confirmed in all animals, both by external and internal, analytical observation. In the teleological theory of nature, an organ that is not intended to be used, an organization that does not achieve its end, is a contradiction. If we stray from that fundamental principle, we no longer have a lawful but an aimlessly playing nature and hopeless chance takes the place of reason's guiding thread.

Second Thesis

In man (as the sole rational creature on earth) *those natural capacities directed toward the use of his reason are to be completely developed only in the species, not in the individual.*[4] Reason in a creature is a faculty to extend the rules and objectives of the use of all of its powers far beyond natural instinct, and it knows no limits to its projects. However, reason itself does not operate on instinct, but requires trial, practice, and instruction in order gradually to progress from one stage of insight to another. Therefore, each individual man would have to live excessively long if he were to make complete use of all his natural capacities; or if nature has given him only a short lease on life (as is actually the case), she requires a perhaps incalculable sequence of generations, each passing its enlightenment on to the next, to bring its seeds in our species to the stage of development that completely fulfills nature's objective. And the goal of his efforts must be that point in time, at least among the ideas of men,[5] since the natural capacities must otherwise be regarded as in large part purposeless and vain. In that case all practical principles would have to be given up, and nature, whose wisdom serves as a fundamental principle in judging all other arrangements, would in the sole case of man have to be suspected of childish play.

Third Thesis

Nature has willed that man, entirely by himself, produce everything that goes beyond the mechanical organization of his animal existence and partake in no other happiness or perfection than what he himself, independently of instinct, can secure through his own reason. Nature does nothing unnecessary and is not prodigal in the use of means to her ends [*Zwecken*]. Since she gave man reason and the freedom of will based on it, this is a clear indication of her objective [*Absicht*][6] as regards his makeup [*Ausstattung*]. Specifically, he should not be led by instinct, nor be provided for and instructed by ready-made knowledge; instead, he should produce everything from himself. Provision for his diet, his clothing, his bodily safety and defense (for which he was given neither the bull's horns, the lion's claws, nor the dog's teeth, but only hands), all amusements that can make life pleasant, even his insight and prudence, indeed, the goodness of his will—all of these should be entirely of his own making. Nature seems here to have taken delight in the greatest frugality and to have calculated her animal endowments so closely—so precisely to the most pressing needs of a primitive existence—that she seems to have willed that if man should ever work himself up from the grossest barbarity to the highest level of sophistication, to inner perfection in his way of thinking and thereby to happiness (as far as it is possible on earth), he alone would have the entire credit for it and would have only himself to thank; it is as if she aimed more at his rational *self-esteem* than at his well-being. For along this course of human affairs a whole host of hardships awaits man. But it appears that nature is utterly unconcerned that man live well, only that he bring himself to the point where his conduct makes him worthy of life and well-being. What will always seem strange about this is that earlier generations appear to carry out their laborious tasks only for the sake of later ones, to prepare for later generations a step from which they in turn can raise still higher the building that nature had in view—that only the most recent generations should have the good fortune to live in the building on which a long sequence of their forefathers (though certainly without any intention of their own) worked, without being able themselves to partake of the prosperity they prepared the way for. But no matter how puzzling this is, it is nonetheless equally as necessary once one assumes that one species of animal should have reason and that as a class of rational beings—each member of which dies, while the species is immortal—it is destined to develop its capacities to perfection.

20

Fourth Thesis

The means that nature uses to bring about the development of all of man's capacities is the **antagonism** *among them in society, as far as in the end this antagonism is the cause of law-governed order in society.* In this context, I understand antagonism to mean men's *unsocial* *sociability,* i.e., their tendency to enter into society, combined, however, with a thoroughgoing resistance that constantly threatens to sunder this society. This capacity for social existence is clearly embedded in human nature. Man has a propensity for *living in society,* for in that state he feels himself to be more than man, i.e., feels himself to be more than the development of his natural capacities. He also has, however, a great tendency to isolate himself, for he finds in himself the unsociable characteristic of wanting everything to go according to his own desires, and he therefore anticipates resistance everywhere, just as he knows about himself that for his part he tends to resist others. Now this resistance awakens all of man's powers, brings him to overcome his tendency towards laziness, and, driven by his desire for honor, power, or property, to secure status among his fellows, whom he neither *suffers,* nor *withdraws from.* In this way, the first true steps from barbarism to culture, in which the unique social worth of man consists, now occur, all man's talents are gradually developed, his taste is cultured, and through progressive enlightenment he begins to establish a way of thinking that can in time transform the crude natural capacity for moral discrimination into definite practical principles and thus transform a *pathologically* enforced agreement into a society and, finally, into a *moral* whole. Without those characteristics of unsociability—which are in themselves quite unworthy of being loved and from which arises the resistance that every man must necessarily encounter in pursuing his self-seeking pretensions—man would live as an Arcadian shepherd, in perfect concord, contentment, and mutual love, and all talents would lie eternally dormant in their seed; men docile as the sheep they tend would hardly invest their existence with any worth greater than that of cattle; and as to the purpose behind man's creation, his rational nature, there would remain a void. Thus, thanks be to nature for the incompatibility, for the distasteful, competitive vanity, for the insatiable desire to possess and also to rule. Without them, all of humanity's excellent natural capacities would have lain eternally dormant. Man wills concord; but nature better knows what is good for the species: she wills discord. He wills to live comfortably and pleasantly; but nature wills that he should be plunged from laziness and inactive comfort into work and hardship, so that he will in turn seek by his own cleverness to pull himself up from them. The natural impulse to do this—the sources of unsociability and of thoroughgoing resistance that give rise to so much evil but also drive men anew toward further exertions of their powers, consequently to diverse development of their natural capacities—indicates the design of a wise creator, not the hand of a malicious spirit who fiddled with the creator's masterful arrangement or enviously spoiled it.

Fifth Thesis

The greatest problem for the human species, whose solution nature compels it to seek, is to achieve a universal **civil society** *administered in accord with the right.* Since it is only in society—and, indeed, only in one that combines the greatest freedom, and thus a thoroughgoing antagonism among its members, with a precise determination and protection of the boundaries of this freedom, so that it can coexist with the freedom of others—since it is only in such a society that nature's highest objective, namely, the highest attainable development of mankind's capacities, can be achieved, nature also wills that mankind should itself accomplish this, as well as all the other goals that constitute mankind's vocation. Thus must there be a society in which one will find the highest possible degree of *freedom under external laws* combined with irresistible power, i.e., a perfectly *rightful civil constitution,*[7] whose attainment is the supreme task nature has set for the human species; for only by solving and completing it can nature fulfil her other objectives with our species. Necessity compels men, who are otherwise so deeply enamoured with unrestricted freedom, to enter into this state of coercion; and indeed, they are forced to do so by the greatest need of all, namely, the one that men themselves bring about, for their propensities do not allow them to coexist for very long in wild freedom. But once in a refuge such as civil society furnishes, these same propensities have the most salutary effect. It is just as with trees in a forest, which need each other, for in seeking to take the air and sunlight from the others, each obtains a beautiful, straight shape, while those that grow in freedom and separate from one another branch out randomly, and are stunted, bent, and twisted. All the culture and art that adorn mankind, as well as the most beautiful social order, are fruits of unsociableness that is forced to discipline itself and thus through an imposed art to develop nature's seed completely.

Sixth Thesis   23

This problem is both the hardest and the last to be solved by the human species. The difficulty that the mere idea of this task places before us is this: Man is *an animal that,* if he lives among other members of his species, *has need of a master.* For he certainly abuses his freedom in relation to his equals, and although as a rational creature he desires a law that establishes boundaries for everyone's freedom, his selfish animal propensities induce him to except himself from them wherever he can. He thus requires a *master* who will break his self-will and force him to obey a universally valid will, whereby everyone can be free. Where is he to find this master? Nowhere but from among the human species. But even he is an animal who requires a master. Thus, begin wherever he will, it is not to be seen how he can obtain a guarantor [*Oberhaupt*] of public justice who will himself be just, whether he seek it in a single person or in a group of several selected for the role. For each of them will abuse his freedom if he has no one above him to apply force in accord with laws. The supreme guarantor [*Oberhaupt*] should be just *in himself* and still be a *man*. This is therefore the hardest task of all; indeed, its perfect solution is impossible; from such warped wood as is man made, nothing straight can be fashioned. Nature only enjoins us to the approximation of this idea.* That it is also the last task to be solved also follows from this: it requires the correct concept of the nature of a possible constitution, great experience during much of the world's course, and above all else a good will prepared to accept that constitution; but it is hard to find three factors such as these together all at once; when it happens, it will only be very late, and after many futile attempts.

24   *Seventh Thesis*

The problem of establishing a perfect civil constitution depends on the problem of law-governed **external relations among nations** *and cannot be solved unless the latter is.* What use is it to work for a law-governed civil constitution among individual men, i.e., for the organization of a commonwealth? The same unsociability that forces men to do so in turn causes every commonwealth to adopt for itself, i.e., as a nation in relation to nations, an unrestricted freedom in its external relations; consequently, one commonwealth must anticipate from others the same evil that oppressed individual men, forcing them to enter into a law-governed civil state. Nature has thus once more used human quarrelsomeness, men's inevitable *antagonism,* even in the large societies and political bodies that are created through it, as a means for discovering a state of calm and security. That is, through wars, through excessive and never remitting preparation for war, through the resultant distress that every nation must, even during times of peace, feel within itself, they are driven to make some initial, imperfect attempts; finally, after much devastation, upheaval, and even complete exhaustion of their inner powers, they are driven to take the step that reason could have suggested, even without so much sad experience, namely, to leave the lawless state of savagery and enter into a federation of peoples. In such a league, every nation, even the smallest, can expect to have security and rights, not by virtue of its own might or its own declarations regarding what is right, but from this great federation of peoples (*Foedus Amphictyonum*)[8] alone, from a united might, and from decisions made by the united will in accord

---

*The role of man is thus quite artificial. How it may be with the inhabitants of other planets and their nature, we do not know, but if we execute this charge of nature, we can well flatter ourselves that we may claim no mean status among our neighbors in the cosmos. It may perhaps be that among them every individual completely fulfills his destiny during his lifetime. But it is otherwise with us; only the species can hope for this fulfillment.

with laws. However fanciful this idea may seem to be—and it was laughed at as such when advanced by an Abbé St. Pierre[9] or a Rousseau[10] (perhaps because they believed its realization was too near)—it is nonetheless the inevitable outcome of the distress that men cause one another, distress that must force nations to just the same decision (however hard it may be for them) to which savage men were so unhappily forced, namely, to give up their brutal freedom and to seek calm and security in a law-governed constitution. All wars are accordingly so many attempts (though not as man's intention, but as nature's objective) to bring about new relations among nations; by the destruction, or at least the dismemberment of old relations, wars cause new bodies to be formed, bodies, however, that themselves will in turn not be able to maintain themselves, either internally or in relation to one another, and must undergo similar revolutions, until finally—partially through the best possible internal organization of the civil constitution, partially through common external agreement and legislation—a state similar to a civil commonwealth is established and can maintain itself *automatically*.   25

[Here three questions arise for our consideration:] Should one expect that by virtue of some *Epicurean* confluence of efficient causes nations, like minute particles of matter randomly colliding with one another, should experiment with all sorts of organizations that will be destroyed by new collisions, until they finally *chance* upon an organization that works, one that can maintain its form (an occurrence that is not very likely to happen)? Or should one instead assume that here nature follows a regular course in leading our species by degrees from the lower stages of animality to the highest stages of humanity, imposing on man an art that is nonetheless his own, and, through this seemingly chaotic arrangement, developing those original natural capacities in a thoroughly law-governed way? Or may one sooner conclude that on the whole all of men's actions and reactions will result in nothing, at least nothing intelligent, that matters will remain as they have always been, and that one cannot say in advance whether or not the strife that is so natural to our species is preparing us for a hell of evils, however civilized our state may be, since this state itself and all previous cultural progress will, perhaps, once more be ravaged by barbarism (a fate that under the rule of blind chance, which is, in fact, one with lawless freedom, man cannot resist, unless one assumes that he secretly follows the guiding thread of nature's wisdom)? These three questions come roughly to this: is it truly rational to assume that nature is *purposive* in its parts but *purposeless* as a whole? What the lawless state did to savages—namely, hold back all of our species' natural capacities until the evil that this placed them under compelled them to leave this state and enter into a civil constitution, in which all those seeds can be developed—barbarous freedom will also do to   26 already established nations. To wit: by expending all of the commonwealth's powers on arming itself against others, by the devastation caused by war, and, still more, by maintaining themselves in constant readiness for war, they hamper progress toward full development of man's natural capacities;[11] however, the evil that arises from this also forces our species to introduce into the intrinsically healthy mutual opposition among states—an opposition that arises from their freedom—a law of equilibrium and an associated power to enforce it and, consequently, a cosmopolitan state in which the security of nations is publicly acknowledged; this state is not totally lacking in *dangers,* so mankind's powers may not slumber, but it is also not lacking in a principle of equality in their mutual action and reaction, so they do not destroy one another. Before this last step (the federation of nations) can be taken—and it is no more than halfway in mankind's formation—human nature must endure the harshest of evils, which pass in disguise as external well-being; and as long as we have not reached this last stage to which our species has still to climb Rousseau was not so far from right in preferring the state of savages. We are, to a high degree, *cultivated* beyond bearing by all manner of social convention and propriety. But we are a long way from being able to regard ourselves as *moral.* For the idea of morality belongs to culture; and yet using this idea only in reference to semblances of morality, e.g., love of honor and outward propriety, constitutes mere civilization. So long, however, as nations expend all their energies on their vain and violent designs, thus continuously inhibiting their citizens' plodding efforts to shape internally their way of thinking [*Denkungsart*],[12] even withholding all support for it, no progress of this sort is to be expected, because the formation of citizens requires a long process of preparation in every commonwealth. All good that is not grafted onto a morally-good character is nothing but illusion and glistering misery. The human race will likely remain in this state until, in the way I have described, it has worked itself out of this chaotic state of national relations.

27   *Eighth Thesis*

One can regard the history of the human species, in the large, as the realization of a hidden plan of nature to bring about an internally, and **for this purpose,** *also an externally perfect national constitution, as the sole state in which all of humanity's natural capacities can be developed.* This thesis is a consequence of the foregoing one. One sees that philosophy also has its chiliastic vision, but one whose occurrence can be promoted by its idea [*Idee*], though only from afar, and it is thus anything but fanciful. The issue, then, is whether experience can uncover something like a course leading to this objective of nature's [*Naturabsicht*]. I say, it reveals *a little of it;* for its cycle appears to require so long a time to complete that the small part of it through which mankind has until now passed allows one to determine the shape of its course and the relations of its parts to the whole with just as little cer-

tainty as we can determine, from all previous astronomical observation, the path of the sun and its entire host of satellites through the
vast system of fixed stars; nonetheless, based on the premise that the
universe has a systematic structure, and from the little that man has
observed, we can justifiably conclude that such a cycle actually exists.
Furthermore, human nature is so constituted as to be incapable of
indifference toward even the most distant epoch through which our
species must go, if only it can be expected with certainty. This is
especially so in the present case, where it appears that we can by our
own rational organization hasten this happy time for posterity. For
this reason its faintest signs of approach will be very important to us.
Nations now stand in such contrived [künstlich] relations to one
another that none can stand any weakening of its internal culture
without losing power and influence in relation to the others; thus, at
least the preservation, if not the progress of this end of nature's [cul-
ture] is fairly well assured by these nations' ambitious designs. Furthermore, civil freedom can no longer be so easily infringed without
suffering after effects in all areas of endeavor, especially trade, in
which event a nation's power in its foreign relations will diminish. But   28
this freedom is gradually expanding. If one hinders the citizen from
pursuing his well-being in whatever ways consistent with the freedom
of others he chooses, one hampers the liveliness of enterprise generally
and, along with it, the power of the whole. Therefore, restrictions on
personal activities will be increasingly abolished and general freedom
of religion will be granted; enlightenment will thus gradually arise,
though folly and caprice will sometimes slip in; it arises as a great
good that must save the human race from even the self-seeking expan-
sionary schemes of their rulers, if the latter just understand what is to
their own advantage. This enlightenment, however, and with it a certain inclination of the heart that the enlightened man cannot fail to
have toward a good that he fully understands, must gradually ascend
to the thrones and even influence principles of government. Although,
for example, our world rulers presently have no money left over for
public educational institutions, or for anything that pertains to what is
best in the world—since everything is already allocated in advance for
future war—they will yet find it to their own advantage at least not to
hinder their people's albeit weak and slow, personal efforts in this
work. In the end, even war gradually becomes not only a very artificial
undertaking, so uncertain for both sides in its outcome, but also a very
dubious one, given the aftermath that the nation suffers by way of an
evergrowing burden of debt (a new invention) whose repayment
becomes inconceivable. At the same time, the effect that any national
upheaval has on all the other nations of our continent, where they are
all so closely linked by trade, is so noticeable that these other nations
feel compelled, though without legal authority to do so, to offer themselves as arbiters, and thus they indirectly prepare the way for the
great body politic [Staatskörper] of the future, a body politic for

which antiquity provides no example. Although this body politic presently exists only in very rough outline, a feeling seems nonetheless to be already stirring among all its members who have an interest in the preservation of the whole, and this gives rise to the hope that, finally, after many revolutions of reform, nature's supreme objective—a universal *cosmopolitan state,* the womb in which all of the human species' original capacities will be developed—will at last come to be realized.

no more wars

29

Ninth Thesis

A philosophical attempt to work out a universal history of the world in accord with a plan of nature that aims at a perfect civic union of the human species must be regarded as possible and even as helpful to this objective of nature's. It is, indeed, a strange and for all appearances absurd scheme to want to write a history based on an idea of how the course of the world must go if it is to approach a certain rational goal; it seems that such an attitude can only result in a *romance.* If one may nonetheless assume that nature does not proceed without a plan and a final objective, even in the play of human freedom, this idea can still be useful; and while we are too shortsighted to penetrate to the hidden mechanism of her workings, this idea may still serve as a guiding thread for presenting an otherwise planless *aggregate* of human actions as a system, at least in the large. For if one begins with *Greek* history—the one through which all other more ancient or contemporaneous histories have been preserved or at least authenticated;* if one follows the influence of the Greeks on the formation and malformation of the body politic of the *Roman* people, who engulfed the Greek nation, and the influence of the Romans on the *barbarians,* who in their turn destroyed the Romans, up to our own time; and if, as episodes, one adds to this the national histories of other peoples, inasmuch as knowledge of them has bit by bit come to us from these enlightened nations; one will discover a course of improvement conforming to rules in the constitutions of the nations on our continent
30   (which will in all likelihood eventually give laws to all others). By focusing everywhere only on civil constitutions and their laws and on the relations among nations—since by virtue of the good they contained they served over long periods of time to elevate and glorify peoples (and along with them the arts and sciences) who were yet in

---

*Only an *educated public,* which has existed from its outset down to our own time, can authenticate ancient history. Beyond it, everything is *terra incognita;* and the history of those peoples living outside it can begin only at the time at which they entered it. This happened with the *Jewish* people through the Greek translation of the Bible at the time of the Ptolemies, without which their *isolated* reports would receive little credence. From there (once this beginning has been properly fixed) one can follow their narratives back. And so it is with all other peoples. The first page of Thucydides (says Hume) is the only beginning of all true history.[13]

That is super racist and elitist

turn overthrown by their inherent deficiencies, always leaving behind a seed of enlightenment that developed more with each revolution, preparing for a succeeding and still higher stage of improvement—one will, I believe, discover a guiding thread that can serve not only to clarify the thoroughly confused play of human affairs, or to aid in the political art of prophesying future changes in and among nations (a use that has already been made of human history, even when it has been regarded as the incoherent product of ungoverned freedom). It will also clear the way for (what, without presupposing a plan of nature, one cannot reasonably hope for) a comforting view of the future, one in which we represent from afar how the human species finally works its way up to that state where all the seeds nature has planted in it can be developed fully and in which the species' vocation here on earth can be fulfilled. Such a *justification* of nature—or, better, of *providence*—is no unimportant motive for adopting a particular perspective in observing the world. For what use is it to laud and recommend observing the majesty and wisdom of creation in the nonrational realm of nature, if that part of the great theatre of supreme wisdom that contains the purpose of all the rest—the history of the human race—should remain an endless reproach to it, the sight of which compels us against our wills to turn our eyes away from it and, since we despair of ever finding a perfectly rational objective in it, brings us to the point of hoping for that end only in another world?[14]

It would be a misunderstanding of my point of view to [believe] that I want this idea of a world history that is to a certain extent led by an *a priori* guiding thread to take the place of *history* as such, whose composition is wholly *empirical*. This idea is only a reflection of what a philosophical mind (which must above all be well versed in history) could attempt to do from another perspective. Besides, the otherwise laudable detail with which men now record the history of their times naturally causes everyone concern as to how after several centuries our distant descendants will come to grips with the burden of history that we shall leave to them. Without doubt they will treasure the history of the most ancient times, whose documents will have long since vanished, but they will treasure them only from the standpoint of what interests them, namely, what peoples and governments have done to contribute to or to impair the objective of cosmopolitanism. To make note of this in order to direct the ambitions of national leaders and their servants to the only means by which they can be honorably remembered even in the most distant future: that can provide some *small* motivation for attempting such a philosophical history. 31

Notes for
*Idea for a Universal History
with a Cosmopolitan Intent*

References to essays in this volume are to page numbers in the *margins*.

1. A. A., VIII 15–31. This essay first appeared in the *Berlinische Monatsscrift,* November, 1784. The relevant portion of the notice reads: "One of Professor Kant's cherished ideas is that the ultimate end of the human race is the attainment of the most perfect civil constitution; and he wishes that a philosophical historian might undertake to give us a history of mankind from this perspective and to point out the extent to which humanity has at different times approached or distanced itself from this end, as well as what is still to be done to attain it." *Gothaische Gelehrte Zeitung,* 1784 (12th Issue, Feb. 11), p. 95.

2. In this essay Kant seems to use the term *"Gattung,"* species, in relation to mankind in those contexts where he wants to consider him only as one natural creature among others.

3. See *Theory and Practice,* 310 and *Perpetual Peace,* 365.

4. See *Spec. Beg. Human History,* p. 110.

5. See Translator's Introduction, p. 16–17, n. 13.

6. See Note on the Text, p. 26.

7. See Note on the Text, p. 26.

8. The Amphyctyonic League was originally a federation of twelve Greek tribes to protect a religious shrine, especially the shrine at Delphi. Philip II of Macedon used the League to sanction his wars of conquest as sacred wars.

9. Abbé Charles-Irenée Castel de St. Pierre (1658–1743), *Projet de paix perpétuelle,* Utrecht, 1713.

10. J.-J. Rousseau, *Extrait du projet de paix perpétuelle d. M. l'Abbé de St. Pierre,* 1760. See *Spec. Beg. Human History,* 110.

11. See *Perpetual Peace,* 345–46.

12. See Note on the Text, p. 26.

13. "Of the Populousness of Ancient Nations" in David Hume, *Essays Moral, Political, and Literary,* ed. Green and Grose, vol. I, p. 414.

14. See *End of All Things,* 336–38.

An Answer to the Question: What is Enlightenment?[1]
(1784)

Enlightenment is man's emergence from his self-imposed immaturity.[2] *Immaturity* is the inability to use one's understanding without guidance from another. This immaturity is *self-imposed* when its cause lies not in lack of understanding, but in lack of resolve and courage to use it without guidance from another. *Sapere Aude!*[3] "Have courage to use your own understanding!"—that is the motto of enlightenment.

Laziness and cowardice are the reasons why so great a proportion of men, long after nature has released them from alien guidance (*naturaliter maiorennes*),[4] nonetheless gladly remain in lifelong immaturity, and why it is so easy for others to establish themselves as their guardians. It is so easy to be immature. If I have a book to serve as my understanding, a pastor to serve as my conscience, a physician to determine my diet for me, and so on, I need not exert myself at all. I need not think, if only I can pay: others will readily undertake the irksome work for me. The guardians who have so benevolently taken over the supervision of men have carefully seen to it that the far greatest part of them (including the entire fair sex) regard taking the step to maturity as very dangerous, not to mention difficult. Having first made their domestic livestock dumb, and having carefully made sure that these docile creatures will not take a single step without the go-cart to which they are harnessed, these guardians then show them the danger that threatens them, should they attempt to walk alone. Now this danger is not actually so great, for after falling a few times they would in the end certainly learn to walk; but an example of this kind makes men timid and usually frightens them out of all further attempts.

Thus, it is difficult for any individual man to work himself out of the immaturity that has all but become his nature. He has even become fond of this state and for the time being is actually incapable of using his own understanding, for no one has ever allowed him to attempt it. Rules and formulas, those mechanical aids to the rational use, or rather misuse, of his natural gifts, are the shackles of a permanent immaturity. Whoever threw them off would still make only an uncertain leap over the smallest ditch, since he is unaccustomed to this kind of free movement. Consequently, only a few have succeeded, by cultivating their own minds, in freeing themselves from immaturity and pursuing a secure course.

But that the public should enlighten itself is more likely; indeed, if it is only allowed freedom, enlightenment is almost inevitable. For even among the entrenched guardians of the great masses a few will always think for themselves, a few who, after having themselves thrown off the yoke of immaturity, will spread the spirit of a rational appreciation for both their own worth and for each person's calling to think for himself. But it should be particularly noted that if a public that was first placed in this yoke by the guardians is suitably aroused by some of those who are altogether incapable of enlightenment, it may force the guardians themselves to remain under the yoke—so pernicious is it to instill prejudices, for they finally take revenge upon their originators, or on their descendants. Thus a public can only attain enlightenment slowly. Perhaps a revolution can overthrow autocratic despotism and profiteering or power-grabbing oppression, but it can never truly reform a manner of thinking;[5] instead, new prejudices, just like the old ones they replace, will serve as a leash for the great unthinking mass.

Nothing is required for this enlightenment, however, except *freedom;* and the freedom in question is the least harmful of all, namely, the freedom to use reason *publicly* in all matters. But on all sides I hear: *"Do not argue!"* The officer says, "Do not argue, drill!" The taxman says, "Do not argue, pay!" The pastor says, "Do not argue, believe!" (Only one ruler in the world[6] says, *"Argue* as much as you want and about what you want, *but obey!"*) In this we have [examples of] pervasive restrictions on freedom. But which restriction hinders enlightenment and which does not, but instead actually advances it? I reply: The *public* use of one's reason must always be free, and it alone can bring about enlightenment among mankind; the *private use* of reason may, however, often be very narrowly restricted, without otherwise hindering the progress of enlightenment. By the public use of one's own reason I understand the use that anyone as a *scholar* makes of reason before the entire *literate world.* I call the private use of reason that which a person may make in a *civic post* or office that has been entrusted to him.[7] Now in many affairs conducted in the interests of a community, a certain mechanism is required by means of which some of its members must conduct themselves in an entirely passive manner so that through an artificial unanimity the government may guide them toward public ends, or at least prevent them from destroying such ends. Here one certainly must not argue, instead one must obey. However, insofar as this part of the machine also regards himself as a member of the community as a whole, or even of the world community, and as a consequence addresses the public in the role of a scholar, in the proper sense of that term, he can most certainly argue, without thereby harming the affairs for which as a passive member he is partly responsible. Thus it would be disastrous if an officer on duty who was given a command by his superior were to question the appropriateness or utility of the order. He must obey. But as a scholar he cannot be justly constrained from making comments about errors in military service, or from placing them before the public for its judgment. The citizen cannot refuse to pay the taxes imposed on him; indeed, impertinent criticism of such levies, when they should be paid by him, can be punished as a scandal (since it can lead to widespread insubordination). But the same person does not act contrary to civic duty when, as a scholar, he publicly expresses his thoughts regarding the impropriety or even injustice of such taxes. 38 Likewise a pastor is bound to instruct his catecumens and congregation in accordance with the symbol of the church he serves, for he was appointed on that condition. But as a scholar he has complete freedom, indeed even the calling, to impart to the public all of his carefully considered and well-intentioned thoughts concerning mistaken aspects of that symbol,[8] as well as his suggestions for the better arrangement of religious and church matters. Nothing in this can weigh on his conscience. What he teaches in consequence of his office as a servant of the church he sets out as something with regard to which he has no discretion to teach in accord with his own lights; rather, he offers it under the direction and in the name of another. He will say, "Our church teaches this or that and these are the demonstrations it uses." He thereby extracts for his congregation all practical uses from precepts to which he would not himself subscribe with complete conviction, but whose presentation he can nonetheless undertake, since it is not entirely impossible that truth lies hidden in them, and, in any case, nothing contrary to the very nature of religion is to be found in them. If he believed he could find anything of the latter sort in them, he could not in good conscience serve in his position; he would have to resign. Thus an appointed teacher's use of his reason for the sake of his congregation is merely *private,* because, however large the congregation is, this use is always only domestic; in this regard, as a priest, he is not free and cannot be such because he is acting under instructions from someone else. By contrast, the cleric—as a scholar who speaks through his writings to the public as such, i.e., the world—enjoys in this *public use* of reason an unrestricted freedom to use his own rational capacities and to speak his own mind. For that the (spiritual) guardians of a people should themselves be immature is an absurdity that would insure the perpetuation of absurdities.

But would a society of pastors, perhaps a church assembly or venerable presbytery (as those among the Dutch call themselves), not be justified in binding itself by oath to a certain unalterable symbol in order to secure a constant guardianship over each of its members and through them over the people, and this for all time: I say that this is 39 wholly impossible. Such a contract, whose intention is to preclude forever all further enlightenment of the human race, is absolutely null and void, even if it should be ratified by the supreme power, by parliaments, and by the most solemn peace treaties. One age cannot bind itself, and thus conspire, to place a succeeding one in a condition whereby it would be impossible for the later age to expand its knowledge (particularly where it is so very important), to rid itself of errors, and generally to increase its enlightenment. That would be a crime against human nature, whose essential destiny lies precisely in such progress; subsequent generations are thus completely justified in dismissing such agreements as unauthorized and criminal. The criterion of everything that can be agreed upon as a law by a people lies in this question: Can a people impose such a law on itself?[9] Now it might be possible, in anticipation of a better state of affairs, to introduce a provisional order for a specific, short time, all the while giving all citizens, especially clergy, in their role as scholars, the freedom to comment publicly, i.e., in writing, on the present institution's shortcomings. The provisional order might last until insight into the nature of these matters had become so widespread and obvious that the combined (if not unanimous) voices of the populace could propose to the crown that it take under its protection those congregations that, in accord with their newly gained insight, had organized themselves under altered religious institutions, but without interfering with those wishing to allow matters to remain as before. However, it is absolutely forbidden that they unite into a religious organization that nobody may for the duration of a man's lifetime publicly question, for so doing would deny, render fruitless, and make detrimental to succeeding generations an era in man's progress toward improvement. A man may put off enlightenment with regard to what he ought to know, though only for a short time and for his own person; but to renounce it for himself, or, even more, for subsequent generations, is to violate and trample man's divine rights underfoot. And what a people may not decree for itself may still less be imposed on it by a monarch, for his lawgiving authority rests on his unification of the people's collective will in his own. If he only sees to it that all genuine or purported improvement is consonant with civil order, he can allow his subjects to do what they find necessary to their spiritual well-being, which is not his affair. However, he must prevent anyone from forcibly interfering with another's working as best he can to determine and promote his well-being. It detracts from his own majesty when he interferes in these matters, since the writings in which his subjects attempt to clarify their insights lend value to his conception of governance. This holds whether he acts from his own highest insight—whereby he calls upon himself the reproach, *"Caesar non est supra grammaticos."*[10]— as well as, indeed even more, when he despoils his highest authority by supporting the spiritual despotism of some tyrants in his state over his other subjects.

If it is now asked, "Do we presently live in an *enlightened* age?" the answer is, "No, but we do live in an age of *enlightenment.*" As matters now stand, a great deal is still lacking in order for men as a whole to be, or even to put themselves into a position to be able without external guidance to apply understanding confidently to religious issues. But we do have clear indications that the way is now being opened for men to proceed freely in this direction and that the obstacles to general enlightenment—to their release from their self-imposed immaturity— are gradually diminishing. In this regard, this age is the age of enlightenment, the century of Frederick.[11]

A prince who does not find it beneath him to say that he takes it to be his *duty* to prescribe nothing, but rather to allow men complete freedom in religious matters—who thereby renounces the arrogant title of *tolerance*—is himself enlightened and deserves to be praised by a grateful present and by posterity as the first, at least where the government is concerned, to release the human race from immaturity and to leave everyone free to use his own reason in all matters of conscience. Under his rule, venerable pastors, in their role as scholars and without prejudice to their official duties, may freely and openly set out for the world's scrutiny their judgments and views, even where these occasionally differ from the accepted symbol. Still greater freedom is afforded to those who are not restricted by an official post. This spirit of freedom is expanding even where it must struggle against the external obstacles of governments that misunderstand their own function. Such governments are illuminated by the example that the existence of freedom need not give cause for the least concern regarding public order and harmony in the commonwealth. If only they refrain from inventing artifices to keep themselves in it, men will gradually raise themselves from barbarism.

I have focused on religious matters in setting out my main point concerning enlightenment, i.e., man's emergence from self-imposed immaturity, first because our rulers have no interest in assuming the role of their subjects' guardians with respect to the arts and sciences, and secondly because that form of immaturity is both the most pernicious and disgraceful of all. But the manner of thinking of a head of state who favors religious enlightenment goes even further, for he realizes that there is no danger to his *legislation* in allowing his subjects to use reason *publicly* and to set before the world their thoughts concerning better formulations of his laws, even if this involves frank criticism of legislation currently in effect. We have before us a shining example, with respect to which no monarch surpasses the one whom we honor.

But only a ruler who is himself enlightened and has no dread of shadows, yet who likewise has a well-disciplined, numerous army to guarantee public peace, can say what no republic[12] may dare, namely: *"Argue as much as you want and about what you want, but obey!"* Here as elsewhere, when things are considered in broad perspective, a strange, unexpected pattern in human affairs reveals itself, one in which almost everything is paradoxical. A greater degree of civil freedom seems advantageous to a people's *spiritual* freedom; yet the former established impassable boundaries for the latter; conversely, a lesser degree of civil freedom provides enough room for all fully to expand their abilities. Thus, once nature has removed the hard shell from this kernel for which she has most fondly cared, namely, the inclination to and vocation for free *thinking,* the kernel gradually reacts on a people's mentality (whereby they become increasingly able to *act freely*), and it finally even influences the principles of *government,* which finds that it can profit by treating men, *who are now more than machines,* in accord with their dignity.*

42

Königsberg in Prussia, 30 September 1784
I. Kant

---

*Today I read in Büsching's *Wöchentliche Nachtrichten* for September 13th a notice concerning this month's *Berlinischen Monatsschift* that mentions *Mendelssohn's* answer to this same question. I have not yet seen this journal, otherwise I would have withheld the foregoing reflections, which I now set out in order to see to what extent two person's thoughts may coincidentally agree.

Notes for
What Is Enlightenment?

References to essays in this volume are to page numbers in the *margins.*

1. A. A., VIII, 33–42. This essay first appeared in the *Berlinische Monatsschrift,* December, 1784.

2. The German is *Unmündigkeit,* which quite literally means "minority," where one is referring to the inability to make decisions for oneself. Kant's point in the essay is that by virtue of understanding and reason men have the inherent right and ability to make all intellectual, political and religious decisions for themselves. That they do not is a function of certain, perhaps implicit, choices they make in regard to exercising rights and developing capacities.

3. "Dare to know!" (Horace, *Epodes,* 1, 2, 40.) This motto was adopted by the Society of the Friends of Truth, an important circle of the German Enlightenment.

4. "Those who have come of age by virtue of nature."

5. The term Kant uses here and later, on p. 41, is *Denkungsart;* it occurs in the second edition preface to the *Critique of Pure Reason,* where he works out his famous analogy of the Copernican Revolution in philosophy, which he refers to as a revolution in the method of thought. (B vii–xxiv) The term refers to one's characteristic pattern of thought, whether it is marked by systematic, rational procedures or by prejudice and superstition, criticism or dogmatism.

6. Frederick II (the Great) of Prussia.

7. See *Theory and Practice,* 304.

8. Kant distinguishes between two classes of concepts, those that we can schematize, i.e., directly represent in experience (intuition), and those that we must symbolize, i.e., indirectly represent in experience (intuition). Symbolized concepts, such as the one we have of God, are those for which no experience can provide adequate content; consequently, experience can only be used to indicate the content we intend. All religious concepts have this character. By symbol in this context, then, Kant means those beliefs and practices in which a group expresses the content of its concept of the divine. (*Crit. Judgment,* 351–54)

9. This would seem a peculiarly political expression of the Categorical Imperative, particularly as it is expressed in *Groundings,* 428–29.

10. "Caesar is not above the grammarians." See *Perpetual Peace,* 368 f.

11. Frederick II (the Great), King of Prussia.

12. The term Kant uses here is *Freistaat,* which is idiomatically translated "republic." However, Kant never again uses this Germanic rooted word in the essays included in this volume. In all the other essays he uses the Latin loan word *Republic*. I point this out because what Kant says here about a *Freistaat* is inconsistent with what he says elsewhere about a *Republic*.

Speculative Beginning of Human History[1]
(1786)

Surely it is permissible *to insert* speculations into the *progression* of a history in order to fill out gaps in the reports, because what comes before, as distant cause, and what follows, as effect, can give a fairly reliable clue for discovering the intervening causes so as to make the transition comprehensible. To produce a history entirely from speculations alone seems no better than to sketch a romance. Thus it could not go by the name of *speculative history* but rather only that of *fiction*. Yet, what may not be ventured regarding the progression of the history of human actions, can nonetheless be attempted through speculation regarding their *first beginnings,* as far as these are made by *nature.* For this speculation need not be fictional, but can instead be based on experience, if one presupposes that in their first beginnings these actions were no better or worse than we now find them to be, a presupposition that conforms to the analogy of nature and has no risky consequences. A history of freedom's first development, from its original capacities in the nature of man, is therefore something different from the history of freedom's progression, which can only be based on reports.

However, since speculations may not make too high a claim on one's assent, they must not lay claim to being serious business, but perhaps rather only to being an exercise of the imagination in the company of reason, carried out for the sake of the mind's relaxation and health. Thus, they cannot compare with those histories that, as actual reports whose verification rests on grounds entirely different from the mere philosophy of nature, set out the very same events and are to be believed as such. Because of that, and because I here undertake a mere flight of fancy [*Luftreise*], I may hope to be granted permission to use a holy document as a map and, at the same time, to imagine that my flight—taken on the wings of imagination, though not without a guiding thread by which, through reason, it is tied to experience —follows precisely the same line as is sketched out in that historical document. If the reader will check the pages of that document (Genesis, 2–6), he can see whether the path that philosophy follows by means of concepts coincides every step along the way with the one set out by history.

If one's speculation is not to wander aimlessly, one must make one's beginning something that human reason is utterly incapable of deriving from any previous natural causes, hence, with the *existence of man.* Indeed, one must begin with man as a *fully formed adult,* for he must do without maternal care; one must begin with a *pair,* so that he can propagate his kind; and one must begin with *only a single pair,* so that war does not arise, as it would if men lived close to one another and were yet strangers, and also in order that nature might not be accused of having erred regarding the most appropriate organization for bringing about the supreme end of man's vocation, sociability [*Geselligkeit*], by allowing differences in lines of descent; for the unity of the family from which all men should descend was without doubt the best arrangement for attaining that end. I put this pair in a place secured against attack by predators, one richly supplied by nature with all the sources of nourishment, thus, as it were, in a *garden,* and in a climate that is always mild. And what is still more, I consider this pair only after it has already taken a mighty step in the skillful employment of its powers; and thus I do not begin with his nature in its completely raw state, for there might easily be too many speculations and too few probabilities for the reader if I were to undertake to fill in this gap, a gap that one must suppose encompasses a great space of time. The first man could thus *stand* and *walk;* he could *talk* (Gen. 2:20),* even *converse,* i.e., speak in coherent concepts (v.23), consequently, *think.* These are skills that he must have developed completely by himself (for were they innate [*anerschaffen*], they would also have to be inherited [*anerben*], which contradicts experience); but I assume him already to possess them so as to consider only the development of morality in his actions and passions, which necessarily presuppose that skillfulness.

111

Instinct—that *voice of God* that all animals obey—must alone have first guided the beginner. This permitted him to use several things for nourishment, but forbade others (Gen. 3:2-3). However, it is not necessary to assume a special, but now lost, instinct for this purpose; it could have been met simply by the sense of smell and its connection with the organ of taste, the latter's acknowledged sympathy with the organs of digestion, and, at the same time, the ability, which we are aware of even at present, to sense beforehand whether something is fit or unfit to be used for food. One need not even assume that this sense was more acute in the first pair than it is now; for the distinction in the powers of perception between those men who are occupied with their senses and those who are also occupied with their thoughts, whereby they disregard their sensations, is well-enough known.

As long as inexperienced man obeyed this call of nature, he was well-served by it. But reason soon began to stir and sought, by means of comparing foods with what some sense other than those to which the instinct was tied—the sense of sight, perhaps—presented to it as similar to those foods, so as to extend his knowledge of the sources of

*While still alone, man must have been moved by the impulse to communicate—at first to make his existence known—to other living beings around him, especially those that make sounds that he could imitate and afterwards use as names. One still sees a similar effect of this impulse in children and thoughtless persons who disturb the thinking members of the commonwealth by rattling, shouting, whistling, singing, and other noisy amusements (the same also occurs in religious devotions). For I can see no other motive for this except that they want to make their existence known far and wide.

nourishment beyond the limits of instinct. If only this attempt had not contradicted nature, it could, with luck, have turned out well enough, even though instinct did not advise it. However, it is a characteristic of reason that it will with the aid of imagination cook up desires for things for which there is not only no natural urge, but even an urge to avoid; at the outset these desires go by the name of greediness[2] [*Lust-ernheit*], and from them arise a whole swarm of unnecessary, indeed even unnatural, propensities that go by the name of voluptuousness [*Üppigkeit*]. The occasion for deserting the natural urges may only have been a petty matter; however, the result of this first attempt, whereby man became conscious of reason as an ability to go beyond   112 those limits that bind all animals, was very important to and even decisive for his way of life. Perhaps a mere fruit whose appearance [*Anblick*] resembled that of others that he had tasted and found agreeable tempted man to experiment; or perhaps it was the example of some animal whose nature was fitted for consuming it, whereas, on the contrary, it was detrimental to man's nature, so that his natural instinct consequently resisted it. Either could have given reason the first occasion to play tricks on the voice of nature (Gen. 3:1), and in spite of the latter's opposition to make a free choice that, as the first, apparently did not have the anticipated outcome. No matter how insignificant may have been the damage done to the voice of nature, man now proceeded with his eyes open (Gen. 3:7). He discovered in himself an ability to choose his own way of life and thus not to be bound like other animals to only a single one. The momentary delight that this just discovered advantage may have awakened in him must have been followed immediately by anxiety and unease as to how he should proceed with this newly discovered ability, for he knew nothing about its hidden characteristics and distant consequences. He stood as if at the edge of an abyss; for besides the particular objects of desire on which instinct had until now made him dependent, there opened up to him an infinitude of them, among which he could not choose, for he had no knowledge whatsoever to base choice on; and it was now equally impossible for him to turn back from his once tasted state of freedom to his former servitude (to the rule of the instincts).

Next to the instinct for nourishment, by which nature preserves each individual, the most dominant is the *instinct for sex,* whereby she cares for the preservation of the species [*Art*]. Once aroused, reason did not hesitate to demonstrate its influence here as well. Man soon found that sexual attraction—which in animals rests on a passing, largely periodic impulse—is capable of being prolonged and even increased by the imagination, which pursues its affairs the more temperately, but at the same time with more obduracy and constancy, the more removed are the objects of the *senses,* and he thereby discovered the weariness that accompanies the appeasement of mere animal desire. The fig leaf (Gen. 3:7) was thus the product of a far greater ex-   113 pression of reason than the one displayed in the first stage of its development. For making a propensity become more internal and obdurate by removing the objects of the senses [from view] already displays consciousness of a certain mastery of reason over the impulses, and not merely, as in the first step, an ability to pay obeisance to them within smaller or greater boundaries. *Refusal* was the feat whereby man passed over from mere sensual to idealistic attractions, from mere animal desires eventually to love and, with the latter, from the feeling for the merely pleasant to the taste for beauty, at first only human beauty, but then also the beauty found in nature. In addition, *decency*—a propensity to influence others' respect for us by assuming good manners (by concealing whatever could arouse the low opinions of others), as the proper foundation of all true sociability—gave the first hint of man's formation into a moral creature. It was a small beginning that was nonetheless epochal, since it gave an entirely new direction to man's way of thinking [*Denkungsart*]; as such, it is more important than the entire, incalculable series of cultural expansions that follow from it.

Reason's third step, after having mixed itself into the first immediately felt needs, was the reflective *expectation of the future*. This ability not merely to enjoy life's present moment but to make present to himself future, often very distant time is the distinguishing characteristic of man's superiority, for in conformity with his vocation he can prepare himself in advance for distant ends [*Zwecken*], though it is at the same time also the most inexhaustible source of cares and troubles, which the uncertain future arouses and from which all animals are exempt (Gen. 3:13-19). The husband, who had to provide his wife and future children with food, foresaw the ever-increasing toilsomeness of his work; the wife foresaw the difficulties to which nature had subjected her sex, as well as the additional ones to which the more powerful husband would subject her. With fear, both foresaw in the background of the picture, at the end of a life of toil, what indeed all animals inevitably face—though without being troubled by it—namely, death, and they seem to have rebuked and made a crime of the use of reason, which caused all these evils to befall them. Perhaps their sole comforting prospect was to live in and through their descendants, or, I should say, to live as members of a family where their burdens would be eased (Gen. 3:16-20).

114

The fourth and final step that reason took in raising mankind altogether beyond any community with animals was that through it he conceived himself (though only darkly) to be the true *end of nature,* and in this regard nothing living on earth can compete with him. The first time he said to the sheep, *"the pelt that you bear was given to you by nature not for yourself, but for me;"* the first time he took that pelt off the sheep and put it on himself (Gen. 3:21); at that time he saw within himself a privilege by virtue of which his nature surpassed that of all animals, which he now no longer regarded as his fellows in creation, but as subject to his will as means and tools for achieving his own chosen objectives. This picture of things includes (however darkly) the thought of its contrary, namely, that he may not speak in this way to any *man* but must regard all men as equal recipients of nature's gifts. This was early preparation for the limitations that reason would in the future place upon him in regard to his fellow man and which is far more necessary to establishing society than inclination and love.

And so man became the *equal of all* [other] *rational beings,* no matter what their rank might be (Gen. 3:22), especially in regard to his claim *to be his own end,* his claim also to be valued as such by everyone, and his claim not to be used merely as a means to any other ends. In this—and not in reason insofar as it is considered merely to be a tool for satisfying his many inclinations—is to be found the basis of the unqualified equality of mankind with higher beings, whose natural endowments may otherwise surpass his beyond all comparison, but who do not for that reason have a right to command him in accord with their own pleasure. This step is at the same time also connected with man's *release* from nature's womb, a change that is, indeed, honorable, but also full of danger, since she drove him out of the safe and secure state of childhood—a garden as it were, that cared for him without his troubling himself (Gen. 3:23)—and threw him into the world, where he was awaited by so many cares, burdens, and unknown evils. In future times, the toilsomeness of life would often arouse in him the hope for a paradise—the creation of his imagina- 115 tion—where he could dream or trifle away his existence in peaceful inactivity and permanent peace. But lying between him and that imagined place of bliss was reason, which restlessly and irresistibly drove him to develop those capacities [*Fähigkeiten*] that lay within him, and it did not allow him to return to that crude and simple state from which it had torn him (Gen. 3:24). It drove him to undertake with patience the toil that he hates, to chase after the frippery that he despises, and to forget death itself, which fills him with horror—all for the sake of those trivialities whose loss he dreads still more.

Remark

This portrayal of mankind's earliest history reveals that its exit from that paradise that reason represents as the first dwelling place of its species was nothing but the transition from the raw state of a merely animal creature to humanity, from the harness of the instincts to the guidance of reason—in a word, from the guardianship of nature to the state of freedom. Whether man has gained or lost as a result of this change can no longer be asked, at least if one looks to the vocation of his species, which consists of nothing other than *progress* toward perfection, no matter how faulty may have been his first attempt, or even the first long series of attempts, to move on toward this goal. For all of that, this path that for the species leads to *progress* from the worse to the better does not do so for the individual.[3] Before reason awoke, there was still neither a command nor a prohibition and thus no transgression either; but as reason took up its business and, weak as it is, came to grips with animality and all its power, then evil and, even worse, the vices of a cultivated reason had to arise, both of which were completely alien to the state of ignorance and, consequently, innocence. Thus, from the moral side, the first step from this last state [the state of innocence] was a *fall;* from the physical side, a multitude of never before known evils of life, thus punishment, was the consequence of this fall. The history of *nature,* therefore, begins with good, for it is God's work; the history of *freedom* begins with badness, for it is *man's* work. For the individual, who in the use of his freedom has regard only for himself, such a change was a loss; for nature, whose end for man concerns the species, it was a victory. Man, therefore, has cause to ascribe to himself the guilt for all the evil that he suffers and for all the bad that he perpetrates, while at the same time, as a member of the whole (the species), admiring and praising the wisdom and purposefulness of the arrangement. In this way one can bring the oft misunderstood and seemingly contradictory claims of the esteemed *J. -J. Rousseau* into agreement with one another and with reason. In his works, *On the Influence of the Sciences* and *On the Inequality Among Men,*[4] he displays with complete accuracy the inevitable conflict between culture and the human race as a *physical* species whose every individual member ought fully to fulfill its vocation. But in his *Emile,* in his *Social Contract,* and in other works he seeks to answer this more difficult question: how must culture progress so as to develop the capacities belonging to mankind's vocation as a *moral* species and thus end the conflict within himself as [a member of both a] moral species and a natural species? From this conflict (since culture founded on true principles for the *education* of men and citizens has not even properly made a beginning, much less been completed) arise all true evil that oppresses human life and all vice that dishonors it;*

116

*I offer the following as only a few examples of the conflict between mankind's striving in regard to his moral vocation, on the one hand, and the unswerving observation of the laws for his raw and animal state that are laid down in his nature, on the other.

Nature has fixed the [beginning of] the period of maturity, i.e., both the urge and the ability to reproduce, at the age of about 16 or 17, an age at which the youngster literally becomes a man in the raw natural state; for at that time he has the ability to provide for himself, to reproduce his kind, and to provide for his wife and progeny. The simplicity of his needs makes this easy. By contrast, in the civilized state, meeting these needs requires many means for making a living and skillfulness, as well also as favorable external circumstances, so that in the civil state this period will on average be reached at least ten years later. Nonetheless, nature has not correspondingly changed the time of its call [so as to cohere] with progress in social refinement, but instead stubbornly follows her law, which was set down for the preservation of the human species as an animal species. Thus, from morals arises a breach with nature's ends, and from nature's ends arises a breach with morals. For natural man is at a certain age already a man, while the civil man (who has not ceased to be natural man) is only a youngster, indeed only a child; thus, one can regard a person of his years (in the civil state) as incapable of providing for himself, much less others of his kind, even though he has the urge and ability and, consequently, has the call of nature to propagate. For nature certainly has not placed in-

117

the impulses to vice, for which man should be given the blame, are, in   117
themselves and as natural capacities, good and serve a purpose. But
since these natural capacities were given man in his natural state, they
will conflict with culture as it proceeds, just as it will conflict with
them until art so perfects itself as to be a second nature, which is the   118
final goal of the human species' moral vocation.

The Resolution of History

The following period began when man passed from the period of
leisure and freedom to that of work and discordant struggle, the
prelude to unification in society. Here we must once more make a
great leap and place man in possession of domestic animals and of
nourishing crops for nourishment that he could increase by sowing
and planting (Gen. 4:2), though the passage from the original state of
the wild hunter and the wandering root digger and fruit gatherer to
this second state may have occurred quite slowly. The feud between
men who had until then lived next to one another in peace must have
arisen at this point, and its result was to separate those who followed
different kinds of lives and to scatter them over the earth. The *life of
the herdsman* is not only the most leisurely but also the most secure,
for there is no lack of fodder in vast unpopulated territories.[6] By contrast *agriculture* or farming is full of toil, dependent on inconstant
weather, and consequently insecure; it also requires permanent housing, ownership of land, and strength sufficient to protect it; the herdsman, however, hates property ownership because it limits his freedom
to pasture [his herds]. The farmer might seem to have envied the
herdsman as being more blessed by heaven (Gen. 4:4), while, in fact,

---

stincts and abilities in living creatures so that they should fight and suppress them. The
capacity for propagation was not placed there for the sake of the civilized state, but
merely for preserving the human species as an animal species; and thus the civilized state
comes into inevitable conflict with the latter, since only a perfect civil constitution
(culture's ultimate aim) could end this conflict, whereas the time until it comes into existence will as a rule be filled with vices and their results, the multiplicity of human
miseries.

Another example to show the truth of the proposition that nature has given man two
different sets of capacities for two different ends—namely, an end for man as animal
species and another end for man as moral species—is to be found in Hippocrates's saying, *Ars longa, vita brevis.* If only a man were to live for an amount of time equal to the
sum of several life spans, and possessed throughout the spiritual vigor of youth, a great
mind with a talent for such things who had once succeeded in reaching full maturity of
judgment through long training and acquisition of knowledge could advance the
sciences and arts much further than entire generations of scholars succeeding one
another. But nature has apparently made its decision regarding the duration of man's
life with things other than the furtherance of the sciences in view. For just when the
most gifted man stands on the brink of the greatest discovery that his skill and experience can allow him to hope for, old age makes its entrance; his mind becomes dull
and he must leave it to a second generation (that must begin again with the ABC's and
must once more travel the entire stretch that had already been covered) to make a small
contribution to culture's progress. It appears, therefore, that the human species' path-

the herdsman annoyed the farmer enormously as long as he remained
119 in the neighborhood, for grazing cattle do not spare the farmer's
crops. Since the herdsman leaves behind nothing of value that he cannot find in other places, it is a simple matter for him to move his herd
to distant parts, once it has done its damage, and in so doing he avoids
having to make good on the damage. (Because these incidents could
not be altogether stopped), it was probably the farmer who first used
force against such invasions, invasions that the herdsman did not
regard as forbidden, and if the farmer did not want to give up the
fruits of his long hours of hard work, he found that he had finally to
remove himself as far as possible from those who followed the herding
life (Gen. 4:16). This separation comprises the third period.

When subsistence depends on the earth's cultivation and planting
(especially trees), permanent housing is required, and its defense
against all intrusions requires a number of men who will support one
another. Consequently, men who adopt this form of life can no longer
remain in scattered families, but must instead come together and
found villages (improperly called *towns*) in order to protect their property against wild hunters or hordes of wandering herdsmen. The
primary needs of life required (Gen. 4:20) by a *different way of living*
could now be *exchanged* for one another. Culture and the beginning
of art, of entertainment, as well as of industriousness (Gen. 4:21–22)
must have sprung from this; but above all, some form of civil constitution and of public justice began, at first, to be sure, only in regard
to the grossest brutality, revenge for which was no longer sought by
the single individual, as it was in the state of savagery, but rather by a
lawful power that preserved the whole, i.e., became a form of government, and was controlled by no other power (Gen. 4:23–24). From
this first, crude structure, all human arts, of which *sociability* and *civil
security* are the most worthwhile, could gradually develop, the human
race could multiply, and from some central point, like a beehive,

---

way to the complete fulfillment of its vocation is to be endlessly interrupted, and the
species is in continual danger of falling back into its old crudeness. And it was not entirely without basis that the Greek philosopher complained, "It is unfortunate that one
must die just when he has begun to have insight regarding how one ought properly to
live."[5]

A third example can be taken from the *inequality* among men, not inequality in
natural gifts or in good fortune, but rather in their rights as humans, an inequality
118 regarding which Rousseau's complaint contains a great deal of truth. But it is an inequality that cannot be separated from culture as long as it proceeds, as it were, without
a plan (which is, in any case, inevitable throughout much of time); however, nature has
certainly not condemned man to this inequality, for she gave him freedom and reason,
and this freedom is not limited by anything except its own universal and external
lawfulness, which is called *civil right*. Man ought to work his own way up from the
crudeness of his natural capacities, and, while he raises himself above them, he should
nonetheless beware not to do them violence. But this is a skill that he cannot expect [to
acquire] until very late and only after many unsuccessful attempts; in the meantime,
humanity suffers from the evils that man inflicts upon himself through lack of experience.

already educated colonists could be sent everywhere. *Inequality among men*—that source of so many evils, but also of everything good—also began during this period and increased later on.

Now as long as nomadic herdsmen, who acknowledged God alone as their ruler, still swarmed about the residents of villages and the farmers, who have a man (government) as their ruler (Gen. 6:4),* and as long as nomads, who are express enemies of the ownership of land, were hostile to those other two groups, and these in turn hated the nomads, there was continual war between them, or at least incessant danger of war, though on both sides people were able to take joy, at least within their own social structures, in that invaluable good, freedom—(for even now danger of war is the only thing that tempers despotism, because wealth is required if a nation is to be powerful, and without *freedom* none of the industriousness that produces wealth will arise. One finds, instead of this industriousness, that poor people must participate to a considerable degree in the preservation of the commonwealth, which would not otherwise be possible except that they feel free within it.) In time, however, the ever rising luxury [enjoyed by] the residents of villages—especially the art of giving pleasure, in which village wives eclipsed the filthy desert girls—must have been a powerful temptation (Gen. 6:2) to those herdsmen to enter into a union with those residents and to allow themselves to be drawn into the glistering misery of the cities. This melding together of two otherwise hostile peoples resulted in an end of all threat of war, as well as the end of all freedom; it also resulted in a despotism of powerful tyrants: these were, on the one hand, a scarcely begun culture abandoned in slavery to a soulless opulence, accompanied by all the vices of man's crude state [of existence], and, on the other, the human race's irresistible urge to depart from the path marked out by nature toward developing its capacities for goodness. And it was thus that man made himself unworthy of existing as a species designated to rule over the earth, and not as one designated to live in bovine contentment and slavish servitude. (Gen. 6:17)

Concluding Remark

The reflective person feels a grief that the unreflective do not know, a grief that can well lead to moral ruination: this is a discontentedness with the providence that governs the entire course of the world; and he feels it when he thinks about the evil that so greatly oppresses the human race, leaving it without (apparent) hope for something better. It is of the greatest importance, however, *to be content with prov-*

*Arabic *Bedouins* still call themselves children of a former *Sheik*, the founder of their tribe (e.g., Beni Haled, etc.). He is by no means their ruler and can exercise no power over them. For in a herding people, where nobody has fixed property that must be left behind, every family that becomes displeased can easily separate itself from the tribe and strengthen another by joining it.

idence (even though it has marked out for us so toilsome a road through this earthly world), partly so that we can always take courage under our burdens and—since we push guilt for those burdens off on fate and not ourselves, who may perhaps be the sole cause of these evils—fix our eyes on that fact and not neglect our own obligation to contribute to the betterment of ourselves.[7]

One must understand that the greatest evil that can oppress civilized peoples derives from *wars,* not, indeed, so much from actual present or past wars, as from the never-ending and constantly increasing *arming* for future war. To this all of the nation's powers are devoted, as are all those fruits of its culture that could be used to build a still greater culture; freedom will in many areas be largely destroyed, and the nation's motherly care for individual members will be changed into pitilessly hard demands that will be justified by concern over external dangers. Yet, would there be even this culture, would there be the close connection among classes within the commonwealth deriving from their mutual economic well-being, would there be the large populations, indeed, would there even be the degree of freedom that still remains, even though severely limited by laws, if the constant fear of war did not necessitate this level of *respect for humanity* from the leaders of nations? Just look at China, which because of its location has no powerful enemy to fear, but only an occasional unforeseen attack and in which every trace of freedom has been wiped out. Thus, at the stage of culture at which the human race still stands, war is an indispensable means for bringing it to a still higher stage; and only after a perfect culture exists (God knows when), would a peace that endures forever benefit us, and thus it is possible only in such a culture. In regard to this point, then, we probably bear the guilt for the evils we so bitterly complain of, and, since culture had scarcely begun, Holy Scripture is completely correct in portraying the melding together of peoples into a society and the complete freedom from external danger [that results from it] as a hindrance to all further culture and as a fall to unredeemable corruption.

122   Man's *second dissatisfaction* with the natural order has to do with the *shortness of life*. But one must have a poor understanding of life's true value if one can still wish that it should be longer than it actually is, for that would only prolong a permanent game of struggling with toil and trouble. Yet one cannot blame those who, because of childish judgment, fear death without loving life, and who, despite their difficulty in bringing the most middling contentment to each day of their existence, nonetheless never have enough days to go through the torment again. If, however, one only considers how many cares torment us in providing the means for so short a life and how much injustice is done in hopes of some future, but quite fleeting enjoyment, then from a rational point of view one must believe that if men could look forward to a life span of 800 or more years, a father's life would be no more secure in his son's hands, or one brother's in another's, or one

friend's in another's [than it is now]; further, one would have to believe that the vices of so long-lived a human race must climb to such heights that they would be worthy of no better fate than to be wiped out by a flood covering the entire earth.

The *third* wish—or, rather, the empty longing (for one is aware that the wished for object can never come to be)—is for the *golden age,* whose vague image the poets praise so highly. In that time we shall be released from all the imagined needs that voluptuousness now piles on us, and there shall be satisfaction with having merely natural needs met, a thoroughgoing equality among men, and peace among them that endures forever—in a word, there shall be the pure enjoyment of a carefree life, dreamt away in idleness, or trifled away in childish play. This longing is stimulated by tales of *Robinson Crusoe* or of trips to the South Sea Islands, or, more generally, by the weariness that a reflective man feels regarding the civilized life when he seeks its worth solely in *enjoyment,* and when reason perhaps reminds him to give his life meaning through action he counteracts that reminder by falling back into idleness. The nihilism of this wish to return to that time of simplicity and innocence is sufficiently shown if one will be instructed by the foregoing picture of the original state: Man cannot maintain himself in it because it did not satisfy him; and were he ever 123 to return to it, he would be still less satisfied with it; he has thus to credit his present toilsome state to himself and to his own choice.

Such a picture of man's history [as we have here] is useful and conducive to his instruction and betterment because it points out [1] that he must not blame providence for the evil that oppresses him; [2] that he is also not justified in ascribing his own transgressions to an original sin committed by his original parents, through which a tendency to similar transgressions was inherited by their descendants (for freely willed actions contain nothing hereditary); [3] that, instead, he must admit what they did as his own act, and must completely credit to himself the guilt for all evil that arose from the first misuse of reason, for he is probably conscious that he would behave in precisely the same way were he in those same circumstances, and his first use of reason (even in the face of nature's advice) would have been to misuse it.[8] If that point about moral evil is taken into account, then properly physical evil can, in the balance of merit and guilt, hardly tip the scales in our favor.

So this is the outcome of a philosophical attempt at setting out man's primordial history: Contentment with providence and with the course of human things as a whole, which do not progress from good to bad, but gradually develop from worse to better; and in this progress nature herself has given everyone a part to play that is both his own and well within his powers.

Notes for
Speculative Beginning of Human History

References to essays in this volume are to page numbers in the *margins*.

1. A. A., VIII, 107–123. *Speculative Beginning of Human History* was first published in the *Berlinische Monatsschrift,* January, 1786. Kant's term here and in the first paragraph is *Mutmassung* and its adjective *mutmasslich,* respectively. This has traditionally been translated as conjecture and conjectural, but such a rendering does not seem coherent with Kant's other writings, especially the *Critique of Pure Reason,* where he defines the Latin loan word *speculativ* as follows: "Theoretical knowledge is *speculative* if it concerns an object, or those concepts of an object, which cannot be reached in any experience. It is so named to distinguish it from the *knowledge of nature,* which concerns only those objects or predicates of objects which can be given in a possible experience." A 634/B 662 – A 635/B 663 In the main in this essay, Kant's use of *mutmasslich* conforms with this definition.

2. The term "greediness" does not fully capture the sense of Kant's term here, *Lusternheit,* by which he means inordinate and consuming concern with the sensual.

3. See *Universal History,* 18–19.

4. In English these are generally referred to as *The First Discourse, Discourse on the Sciences and Arts,* and *The Second Discourse, Discourse on the Origin and Foundations of Inequality.* See Jean-Jacques Rousseau, *The First and Second Discourses,* ed. Roger D. Masters, trans. by Roger D. and Judith R. Masters, St. Martin's Press, 1964.

5. We do not know to which Greek Philosopher Kant was referring here.

6. See *Perpetual Peace,* 363 ff.

7. See *Theory and Practice,* 310, *End of All Things,* 337, and *Perpetual Peace,* 360 ff.

8. [3] is an ingenious view of original sin; see *End of All Things,* 331.

On the Proverb: That May be True in Theory, But Is of No Practical Use[1]
(1793)

An aggregation of rules, even of practical rules, is called a *theory,* as long as these rules are thought of as principles possessing a certain generality and, consequently, as being abstracted from a multitude of conditions that nonetheless necessarily influence their application. Conversely, not every undertaking [*Hantierung*] is a *practice* [*Praxis*]; rather, only such ends as are thought of as being brought about in consequence of certain generally conceived [*vorgestellten*] principles of procedure [*Verfahrens*] are designated practices.

Between theory and practice, no matter how complete the theory may be, a middle term that provides a connection and transition is necessary. For to the concept of the understanding that contains the rule must be added an act of judgment by means of which the practitioner decides whether or not something is an instance of the rule. And since further rules cannot always be added to guide judgment in its subsumptions (for that could go on infinitely), there can be theoreticians who, lacking judgment, can never be practical in their lives, e.g., physicians or jurists, who, having done well in school, do not know how they should respond when they are asked for advice.[2] But even where this natural gift is found, premises can still be lacking; that is, the theory can be incomplete, and perhaps it can only be completed by further experiment and experience, from which, then, the newly schooled physician, agriculturist, or economist can and should abstract new rules to complete his theory. Thus, it was not the fault of the theory if it was of little use in practice, but rather of there being *not enough* theory, theory that a man should have learned from experience; and this is true theory, even if he cannot set it out and, as a teacher, expound it systematically in general propositions and, consequently, cannot claim the title of theoretical physician, agriculturist, and so on. Thus nobody can claim himself to be practically proficient in a science and yet disdain its theory without revealing himself to be an ignoramus in his area; for he believes that he can go further by stumbling about in experiments and experience—without putting together certain principles (which properly make up what one calls theory) and without having an overview of his business (which, when pursued methodically, is called a system)—than theory will allow him to go.

Yet it is still easier to excuse an ignorant person who claims that theory is unnecessary and dispensable in his supposed practice, than to excuse a Sophist who concedes its value to the schools (as, perhaps, only a mental exercise) but who at the same time maintains that matters are quite different in practice—that as one leaves school to enter the world, one will realize one has been pursuing empty ideals and philosophical dreams—and, in a word, that what sounds good in theory is of no practical use. (One also often expresses this in the following way: "this or that proposition is indeed valid *in thesi,* but not *in hypothesi.*") Now if the empirical engineer were to say of general mechanics, or an artilleryman of the mathematical doctrine of ballistics that its theory was indeed nicely thought out but was, nonetheless, utterly invalid in practice—since its application in experience gives results wholly different from those [predicted] in theory—one would only laugh (for if one added to the first the theory of friction and to the latter the theory of air resistance—consequently, if one only added still more theory—both would completely agree with experience.) Still, the matter is quite different with a theory concerning objects of intuition than with one in which objects are only represented by concepts (as with objects of mathematics and objects of philosophy). The latter can very probably and without criticism be *thought,* yet it may be quite impossible for them to be given; instead, they may be mere empty ideas that have either no practical use whatsoever or even one that would be disadvantageous. In such cases, therefore, that proverbial saying could be perfectly correct.

But concern over the empty ideality of concepts completely disappears in a theory based on the *concept of duty.* For it would not be a duty to pursue a certain effect of our will (whether it is thought of as completed or as continually approaching completion), if it were not possible to do so in experience, and this is the only kind of theory we are considering in this essay. For it is a scandal to philosophy that we frequently hear advanced the view that what may be true regarding the concept of duty is in fact useless in practice. Indeed, this is said in a lofty, disdainful tone of voice, full of the arrogant desire to use experience to reform reason in that very area in which reason finds its highest honor. And this benighted wisdom believes it can penetrate further and more clearly with its mole-like eyes fixed on experience than with eyes belonging to a being created to stand erect and gaze at the heavens.

This maxim, common in our glib and actionless times, does the greatest harm when directed toward moral matters (to moral or legal duty). For here we are concerned with the canon of reason (in practical matters), where the worth of practice rests entirely on its appropriateness to its underlying theory. All is lost when empirical and therefore contingent conditions of the application of law are made conditions of the law itself, and a practice calculated to effect a result made probable by *past* experience is thus allowed to predominate over a self-sufficient theory.

I divide this essay in accordance with the three different standpoints from which a gentleman[3] who boldly criticizes theories and systems usually judges his objects, thus from three attitudes: (1) the private person who is yet a *man of affairs;* (2) the *statesman;* (3) the *man of the world* (or citizen of the world in general). These three persons are of one mind in going after the *academician,* who concerns himself with theory on their behalf and for their good; but since they imagine themselves to understand this better than he, they desire to banish him to his academy (*illa se iactet in aula!*) as a pedant, who, unfit for practice, only stands in the way of experienced wisdom.

Thus, we shall present the relationship of theory to practice in three sections: *first,* in *morality* in general (in relation to the well-being of each *man*); *second,* in *politics* (in relation to the well-being of *nations*); *third,* in *cosmopolitan* perspective (in relation to the well-being of the *human race* as a whole and insofar as its well-being is conceived as progressing through a sequence of developments during all future times). For reasons that derive from the essay itself, the titles of the sections express the relationship of theory to practice in *morality, political right* and *international right.* 278

I.

On the Relation of Theory to Practice in Morality in General

(In Reply to Some Objections by Prof. Garve*)

Before I proceed to the central point of the controversy over what in the use of one and the same concept may be valid only in theory or only in practice, I must compare my theory, as I have presented it elsewhere, with the presentation Herr Garve has given it, so as to see at the outset whether we understand one another.

A. By way of introduction, I provisionally defined morality as a science that teaches, not how we can be happy, but how we ought to become worthy of happiness.† At the same time I did not fail to remark that man is not expected to *renounce* his natural end, happiness, when the issue of obeying his duty arises; for he cannot do that, no more than any finite rational being in general can. Yet he must completely *abstract* from such considerations when the command of duty

---

Versuche über verschiedene Gegenstände aus der Moral und Literatur [*Essays on Various Topics from Morality and Literature*], by Ch. Garve, Part One, pp. 111–116. I call this worthy man's disagreements with my propositions *objections,* regarding which he desires (I hope) to reach an understanding with me. I do not call them attacks, which are disparaging assertions that arouse defense, for which there is here neither the place nor the inclination.

† The worthiness to be happy is a quality of a person that depends on the subject's very own will, a quality by virtue of which that person's ends will be in complete harmony with a universally legislating reason (a reason that legislates both for nature and for free wills). It is therefore completely different from the skill of producing happiness. For a person is not worthy of this skill nor of the talents with which nature has endowed him if he has a will that does not harmonize with and cannot be included in that will that alone conforms to the universal legislation of reason (i.e., if his will is in conflict with morality).[4]

279 arises, and he must never make happiness the *condition* of obeying the law that reason prescribes for him. Indeed, to the extent possible, he must seek to become conscious that no *motive* deriving from happiness is unknowingly intermixed with his determination of his duty, something that often occurs because we unfortunately represent duty as bound up with the sacrifices its observance (virtue) involves, rather than with the benefits it bestows on us. We must represent the command of duty in its entirety, as requiring unconditional obedience, as sufficient in itself, and as requiring no other influences.

a. Now Herr Garve expresses my proposition in this way: "I had maintained that the observation of the moral law, independently of all considerations of happiness, is the *sole ultimate end* of men, that it must be regarded as the Creator's sole end." (According to my theory neither human morality alone nor happiness alone is the Creator's end; instead, that end is the highest good possible in the world, which consists of the union and harmony of the two.)

B. I further remarked that this concept of duty does not have to be based on any special end, but rather that it *introduces* another end for the human will, namely, to strive with all one's powers toward the *highest good* possible in the world (the purest morality throughout the world combined with such universal happiness as accords with it). Since it is, indeed, within our power to approach this end from one though not from both directions at once, reason is for practical purposes to believe in a moral ruler of the world and in a future life. The universal concept of duty does not first gain "support and stability," i.e., a secure basis and the required force of a *motive,* from the presupposition of these two [human ends]; instead, with this presupposition one only comes to have an *object* for the ideal of pure reason.* For in itself, no matter what the will's object or end may be 280 (consequently, even happiness), duty is nothing other than the will's *limitation* to the requirements of a universal legislation that is made

---

*The need to assume a *highest good* in the world, which is the ultimate end of all things brought about with our coöperation, is not a need deriving from a deficiency in moral motives, but one deriving from a deficiency in those external conditions in which alone an object as an end in itself (as a morally ultimate end) that conforms with these motives can be produced. For in the absence of all ends there can be no will, although when it is merely a matter of compelling an action legally, one must abstract from all 280 ends and make the law alone the determining ground of the will. But not every end is moral (e.g., the end of one's own happiness is not); the moral end must be an unselfish one. And the need for an ultimate end that is set out by pure reason and that includes the totality of all ends within a single principle (a world as the highest good possible through our coöperation) is a need felt by an unselfish will that *extends* beyond the observation of formal laws in bringing its object (the highest good) into existence. This is a special kind of determination of the will, namely, one that derives from the idea of the totality of all ends, the basis of which is that *if* we stand in certain moral relations to things in the world, we must everywhere obey the moral law; beyond this, there is a further duty to strive with all one's abilities to ensure *that* such a relationship (a world conforming to the highest moral ends) exists. In this way man thinks of himself on an analogy with the deity, which, while subjectively needing no external [independently existing] thing, can nonetheless not be thought of as enclosed within itself, but rather as

possible by adopting a maxim; however, [in adopting this maxim] one completely abstracts from both happiness and from every other end that one may have.[6] Thus, where the question of the *principle* of morality is concerned, the doctrine of the *highest good* as the final end of a will that is determined by it and conforms to its laws can be completely disregarded and set aside (as episodic). As will become apparent in what follows, the crucial issue at stake here concerns the principal of morality not at all, but only the universal moral point of view.

  b. Herr Garve expresses the foregoing propositions as follows: "the virtuous man can never, and may never, lose sight of this consideration (his own happiness), since he would otherwise completely lose his [means of] passage to the invisible world and of conviction in God's existence and in immortality, which are, according to this [Kant's] theory necessary to *provide the system of morality with support and stability.*" He concludes with this brief summary of the contentions he attributes to me. "According to these principles, the virtuous man strives unceasingly to be worthy of happiness, but *insofar as* he is truly virtuous, he never strives to be happy." (The word "insofar as" creates an ambiguity here that must be eliminated before all else. It can mean, *in the act,* since he submits to duty as a virtuous man; and this sense agrees completely with my theory. Or it can mean, if he is wholly virtuous, that the virtuous man should not give happiness any consideration whatsoever, even where such consideration is neither forbidden by nor contrary to duty; and that completely contradicts my statements.)

  These exceptions are thus nothing but misunderstandings (for I have no desire to regard them as misinterpretations), whose possibility would be puzzling if such a phenomenon were not explained by the human tendency to follow one's own customary patterns of thought, even in the evaluation of the thoughts of others, and so to impose the former on the latter.

  Garve follows this polemical handling of the foregoing moral principle with a dogmatic assertion to the contrary. Herr Garve draws this analytic conclusion: "In the *conceptual* order of things, states must be perceived and distinguished so that one of them can be given *preference* above the others before a person can proceed to choose among them and, consequently, before one can settle on a certain end. But a

281

---

determined by the consciousness of its complete self-sufficiency to bring about the highest good outside itself. *We* can only represent this necessity (which is duty for men) as if it were a moral need of the supreme being.[5] For man, therefore, the motive contained in the idea of the highest possible good in the world attainable with his coöperation is not the happiness he intends for himself, but only this idea [of the highest good] as an end in itself and of his pursuit of it as his duty. For it does not straightforwardly include the prospect of happiness, but includes it only as a function of a proportion between happiness and the subject's worthiness of it, whatever that may be. But a determination of the will that in itself and in its intention is restricted to the condition of belonging to such a totality is *not selfish.*

state that is *preferred* to other states of being by a creature endowed with consciousness of itself and of its state is, when this state is present and perceived by that creature, a *good* state; and a series of such good states is the most general concept expressed by the term *happiness."* Further: "A law presupposes motives, and motives in their turn presuppose a previously perceived difference between a worse state and one that is better. This perceived difference is the element of the concept of happiness, etc." Furthermore: *"The motives behind every effort arise from happiness* in the most general sense of the term, including compliance with the moral law. I must first know in general whether something is good before I can ask whether fulfillment of moral duties falls under the rubric of the good. Man must have an *incentive* to set him in motion *before* he can establish a goal* towards which this motion should be directed."

This argument involves nothing more than a play on the ambiguity of the term "the good." For it can mean either something unconditionally good in itself, in contrast with something evil in itself, or something only conditionally good by comparison with something that is a lesser or greater good, since the state chosen may only be one that is comparatively better but nonetheless evil in itself. The maxim to abide by a categorically commanded law of free will (i.e., duty)—an adherence that takes no account whatsoever of an end as its basis—is essentially distinct, i.e., distinct in *kind,* from a maxim for a certain way of acting whose motive is an underlying end bestowed by nature itself (the end called happiness in its most general sense). For the first is good in itself, while the latter is by no means so, since in a case where it clashes with duty it can be extremely evil. By contrast, if a certain end is made basic, and consequently no law is commanded unconditionally (except under the assumption of this end as a condition), two contrary actions can both be conditionally good, with one merely better than the other (in which case the latter would be called comparatively evil), for they are distinguished from one another only by *degree,* not in *kind.* And so it is with all actions whose motive is not the unconditioned law of reason (duty), but some end that we have arbitrarily set out as the basis of action; for such an end belongs to the sum of all ends whose attainment is called happiness. And one action can conduce more, another less, to my happiness, and can thus be better or worse than the other. But *the preference* of one state over some other one in the determination of the will [*Willensbestimmung*] is merely an act of freedom (*res merae facultatis,*[8] as lawyers say), in which no attention whatsoever is paid to whether this (determination of the will) is good or evil in itself, and in this regard both states are equivalent.

---

*This is, indeed, precisely what I urge. The incentive that man can have before he sets a goal (end) for himself can be nothing other than the law itself, just because it inspires respect (regardless of the ends one may have and may attempt to achieve by complying with it). For, with regard to the formal aspect of willing, the law is all that remains when I disregard willing's material aspect (the goal, as Herr Garve calls it).[7]

282

A state of being closely associated with a certain *given end* that I   283
prefer over others of the *same kind* is, in the realm of happiness, a
comparatively better state (one that *reason* never recognizes to be
other than conditionally good, insofar as one is worthy of it). But in
cases of conflict between my ends and the moral law, the state that I
consciously prefer from motives of duty is not merely a better one, but
the only one that is good in itself. This good belongs to a wholly different realm, one where no consideration whatsoever is given to the
ends (consequently to their sum, happiness) that may present themselves to me, and where the maxim that is the determining ground
[*Bestimmungsgrund*] of the will is not material (some object on which
it is based) but is rather the mere form of universal lawfulness. Thus,
it can in no way be said that every state I *prefer* to all others is regarded by me as happiness. For I must first be certain that I do not act
contrary to my duty; only then am I allowed to look toward such happiness as I can make compatible with my morally (not physically)
good state.*

Certainly the will must have *motives;* but these are not particular
pre-established ends that are objects to which we relate through
physical feelings; instead, they are nothing but the unconditioned law
itself, and the will's receptivity to finding itself subject to it as to an
unconditioned constraint is called the *moral sense.* Thus, this feeling is
not the cause but the effect of the determination of the will, and we
would not have any perception of this feeling whatsoever if that constraint did not precede it. Therefore, that old litany—namely, that this   284
feeling, consequently a pleasure that we set out as an end, is the first
cause of the will's determination and that, as a result, happiness (of
which that pleasure is an element) is, indeed, the basis of all objective
necessity in action and hence of all obligation—is a trifling sophistry.
If one cannot cease asking questions after a cause has been proposed
for a particular effect, one will finally make the effect the cause of
itself.

I now come to the point that properly concerns us here, namely, to
provide examples of and to test the conflict between theory and practice that supposedly arises in philosophy. Herr Garve gives the best example in the essay of his that we cited above. He says first (referring to
the distinction I find between a doctrine about how we are to become
happy and one as to how we are to become *worthy* of happiness):

*Happiness consists of everything (but nothing more than) nature vouchsafes us; vir-
tue, however, consists of what no one but man can give to or take from himself. If one
were to demur and say that by failing to be virtuous a man can at least incur blame and
pure moral self-reproach, thus self-dissatisfaction, and can as a result make himself
unhappy, we might assuredly agree. But only the virtuous man, or one who is on the
way to it, is capable of suffering this pure moral dissatisfaction (which does not arise
from any disadvantageous results of his actions, but from their very contrariness to
law). Consequently, this feeling is not the cause but the effect of his virtuousness, and
the motivation to be virtuous cannot be derived from this unhappiness (if one so
chooses to name regret over a misdeed).

"For my part, I admit that while I easily conceive this division of ideas in my *head,* I cannot find this division of wishes and strivings in my *heart,* and it is inconceivable to me how any man can be conscious of having completely separated himself from his desire for happiness and of thus having performed his duty altogether unselfishly."[9]

I shall answer the last point first. I readily concede that no man can with certainty be conscious of *having performed* his duty altogether unselfishly. For this is a matter of inner experience, and such an awareness of one's state of mind [*Seelenzustandes*] would involve an absolutely clear representation of everything pertaining to those notions and considerations that imagination, habit, and inclination conjoin to the concept of duty. This is too much to ask for. Moreover, something's nonexistence (even an unconsciously intended advantage) cannot be an object of experience. But that a man *ought to perform* his duty entirely unselfishly and *must* completely separate his desire for happiness from his concept of duty so as to preserve its purity is something of which he is most clearly conscious. Or, if he believes that he is not clearly conscious of it, he can, to the extent that his abilities permit, be required to become so. And he must be capable of having such a consciousness of it, for the true value of morality lies in the purity of its concept. Perhaps there has never been a man who has altogether unselfishly (without admixture of other incentives) performed his acknowledged and revered duty; perhaps no one will ever succeed in doing so, even with the greatest effort. But everyone is capable of rigorous self-examination and can perceive himself becoming conscious not just of the absence of such contributing motives [for happiness], but even more of self-denial regarding many motives that conflict with the idea of duty and thus with the maxim of striving toward that purity [in one's concept of duty]. And that is sufficient for the observation of his duty. On the other hand, to make a maxim of favoring the influence of such motives [for happiness] on the pretense that human nature does not permit such purity (a contention that cannot be maintained with certainty) is the death of all morality.[10]

Now as for Herr Garve's previously quoted confession that he does not find that distinction (more properly separation) in *his heart,* I have no misgivings about straightforwardly contradicting his self-accusation and in taking the side of his heart against his head. He—the honest man—has always actually found the distinction in his heart (in determining his will). It was only in his head—for speculative purposes and in order to conceive the inconceivable (the inexplicable), namely, the possibility of categorical imperatives (such as those of duty)—that the distinction could not be reconciled with the customary principles of psychological explanation (all of which are based on the mechanism of natural necessity).*[11]

*(In his remarks on *Cicero's* book on duties, p. 63, edition of 1783),[12] Herr Professor Garve makes this notable comment, which is witness to his own acuity: "Freedom, according to his innermost conviction, would always remain unresolved and never be ex-

But I must loudly and passionately contradict Herr Garve when he concludes: "In *reflecting* on particular objects, such fine distinctions among ideas become *obscure* and they *completely disappear* when it comes to *action,* where they should apply to desires and intentions. The simpler, faster, and more *stripped of clear representations* is the step by which we proceed from considering our motives for actually acting, the less becomes the possibility for precisely and certainly knowing the specific weight each motive had in guiding that step just so, and not otherwise." 286

In its utter purity, the concept of duty is incomparably simpler and clearer—and everyone can more readily and naturally use it in practice —than is any motive derived from happiness, or one either mixed with happiness or with considerations of it (whose application always involves much skill and reflection). Besides, in the judgment of even the most common human understanding, when the concept of duty alone —separated from and contrasted with these other motives—is presented to the wills of men, then it is far more *powerful,* penetrating, and promising of results than are all the grounds of action [*Bewegungsgründe*] derived from that selfish principle [of happiness]. Let us consider, for example, the case of someone who holds in trust for another person some property (*depositum*) whose owner is dead and whose rightful heirs do not know of and cannot discover its existence. Present this case to a child of say eight or nine years, and suppose even that the property's trustee (through no fault of his own) has at this very time undergone a complete collapse in his fortunes, that he sees around him his family, both wife and children, made miserable by oppressive need, from which need they could be instantaneously relieved if he appropriated that trust to himself. Suppose further that he is philanthropic and charitable, while the heir is rich, misanthropic, and lives luxuriously and wastefully in the highest degree so that the addition of the entrusted deposit to the heir's property would make as little difference as it would if it were thrown into the sea. Without doubt the person questioned [as to the rightness of the trustee's appropriating the trust] will answer, No!, and in lieu of all reasons, he can say only that *it is not right,* i.e., it conflicts with duty. Nothing is clearer than this, even though it is surely not true that the trustee would not promote his own happiness by surrendering the deposit. For if he were of a mind to expect considerations of happiness to determine his decision, he could, for example, reason as follows: If you decide unasked to give the true owners their property, they will 287

plained." A proof of its actuality can never be found at all, neither in direct nor in indirect experience, and lacking all proof, one cannot just assume it. Since a proof of it cannot be derived from mere theoretical grounds (for these must be sought in experience), nor, therefore, from mere practical propositions of reason, nor even from practical propositions in the technical sense (for these would also require an experiential basis), it can come only from morally practical propositions; and so one must wonder why Herr Garve did not resort to the concept of freedom in order to salvage at least the possibility of such imperatives.

probably reward you for your honesty, or if that does not happen, you will acquire a widely known good name, which could become very profitable to you. But all of this is very uncertain, and many considerations can be brought against it: If you were to keep silent about the trust in order at once to relieve yourself of your depressed circumstances, then if you make too sudden use of it, you would subject yourself to suspicion as to how and by what means you had so readily come into your improved circumstances; but if you were to use it slowly, your destitution would in the meantime become so great as to be utterly insurmountable. In reaching its decision, a will whose maxim is grounded in happiness thus vacillates between two incentives, for it looks to the results of its choice, and they are quite uncertain. It takes a good head to find a way out of these arguments and counter-arguments and not to be deceived in the final summing up. By contrast, if a person asks himself what his duty in this situation is, there is no confusion at all regarding the answer he is to give himself, and he is certain on the spot as to what he has to do. Indeed, if the concept of duty has any validity for him, he will feel disgust at calculating the advantages that could accrue to him through its violation, just as if he still had the choice.

That these distinctions (which, as we have just shown, are not so fine as Herr Garve believes, but are etched on the human soul in the firmest and most legible hand), as he says, *completely disappear when it comes to action* is contradicted by his own experience—but not, of course, such experience as the *history* of maxims derived from one or another principle provides, for experience unfortunately demonstrates that the greatest number of such maxims flow from the principle of selfishness. But it contradicts only the inward experience that no idea more elevates and inspires enthusiasm in the human mind than that of pure moral conviction, which reveres duty above all else, struggles with life's countless evils, even its most seductive temptations, and nonetheless conquers all (for we may rightly assume that man can do so). That man is aware that he can do this because he ought to reveals deep tendencies toward the divine that allow him to feel a sacred awe regarding the greatness and sublimity of his true vocation. And if man were to take notice of this vocation more often, were to become accustomed to divesting virtue completely of all the rich loot of advantages to be gained by observing duty, and were to represent it in its complete purity—if it were made a principle of private and public instruction to make constant reference to this attitude (a method of instilling duties that is almost always neglected)—man's moral state would soon improve. That the good consequences of the doctrines of virtue have not so far been demonstrated in our historical experience is probably due to the false assumption that the idea of an incentive derived from duty in itself is too subtle for the common conception of things [*gemeinen Begriffe*]. By contrast, [persons have assumed that] the cruder incentive of expecting certain benefits in this as well as in a future world to follow from obeying the law (without considering the latter as an incentive) would more powerfully affect the mind. And until now the fundamental proposition underlying education and homiletics has been that men prefer happiness to that which reason makes its highest condition, namely the worthiness to be happy. The prescriptions for how one can become happy, or at least for how one can avoid what is disadvantageous, are not *commands*. They bind no one absolutely, and having been warned, one may do what one believes to be good, given that one is prepared to accept the consequences. One has no reason to regard as punishment the evil that might befall one as a result of failing to follow advice that has been offered; for punishment is reserved exclusively for free, but unlawful wills. Nature and inclination cannot set forth laws for freedom. It is completely different with the idea of duty, whose violation, even without the consideration of its resultant disadvantages, affects the mind directly and makes man in his own eyes reprehensible and subject to punishment.

Here, then, is clear proof that everything true in theory for morals must also be valid in practice. In that quality by virtue of which man is a being subject through his own reason to certain duties, everyone is also a *man of affairs*. And since, as human, one never emerges from the school of wisdom, one cannot arrogantly and contemptuously relegate the advocate of theory to the schools, contending that experience better instructs us as to what man is and as to what can be required of him.[13] For all of this experience does not in the least help one   289
to free oneself from the precepts of theory, but at most only to learn how better and more generally to apply it after one has assimilated it into one's fundamental principles. But our concern here is not with pragmatic skills, but only with those principles.

On the Relation of Theory to Practice
in Constitutional Right

(Against Hobbes)

Among all the contracts by which a multitude of men unite themselves into a society (*pactum sociale*), the contract establishing a civil constitution (*pactum unionis civilis*) is of so unique a kind that although in regard to its *execution* it does indeed have much in common with all other contracts (that are similarly directed toward some chosen end promoted by joint effort), it is in principle essentially different from all others in what it founds (*constitutionis civilis*). Uniting many for some (common) end (that they all *have*) is a property of all social contracts; but as an end in itself (that each of them *ought to have*) and, consequently, as an end that is an unconditioned and primary duty with respect to every external relation in general among men, who cannot help but mutually influence one another, this union is met with only in society, and then only insofar as it finds itself in a civil state [*bürgerlichen Zustande*], i.e., constitutes a commonwealth [*gemeines Wesen*].[14] Now in such external relations the end [whose pursuit] is in itself a duty and that is the supreme formal condition *(conditio sine qua non)* of all other external duty is the *right* [*Recht*] of men *under public coercive law,* through which each can receive his due and can be made secure from the interference of others.

The concept of an external right in general derives entirely from the concept of *freedom* in the external relations among men and has nothing whatsoever to do with the ends that men have from nature (the objective of attaining happiness), or with setting out the means for achieving them; and, thus, these latter ends must never be inter-mixed as determining grounds with those laws. *Right* is the limitation of each person's freedom so that it is compatible with the freedom of everyone, insofar as this is possible in accord with a universal law; and *public right* is the totality [*Inbegriff*] of *external laws* that makes such a thoroughgoing compatibility possible. Now since every limitation of freedom by the will [*Willkür*] of another is called coercion, it follows that the civil constitution is a relation among *free* men (notwithstand-ing their complete freedom in uniting with others) who yet stand under coercive laws, for reason itself—indeed, pure *a priori* law-giving reason, which takes no notice of any empirical ends (which can all be grasped under the general name of happiness)—wills it so.[15] As regards happiness, men do have different thoughts about it and each places it where he wants, and hence their wills cannot be brought under any common principle, nor, consequently, under any external law compatible with the freedom of everyone.

Regarded merely as a state of right, the civil state is based *a priori* on the following principles:

1. The *freedom* of every member of society as a
    human being.
2. The *equality* of each member with every other as
    a *subject.*
3. The *independence* of every member of the commonwealth
    as a *citizen.*[16]

These principles are not so much laws set out by an already established nation as they are pure rational principles of external human right in general, in accordance with which alone a nation can be established. Thus:

1. I express the principle of one's *freedom* as a human being in this formula: No one can compel me (in accordance with his beliefs about the welfare of others) to be happy after his fashion; instead, every person may seek happiness in the way that seems best to him, if only he does not violate the freedom of others to strive toward such similar ends as are compatible with everyone's freedom under a possi-ble universal law (i.e., this right of others). A government that was

established on the principle of regarding the welfare of the people in the same way that a father regards his children's welfare, i.e., a *paternal government* (*imperium paternale*)—where the subjects, like *immature* children unable to distinguish between what is truly useful or harmful to them, would be compelled merely to behave passively, merely to await the judgment of the nation's head as to how they *ought* to be happy, and merely to expect his goodness in also willing it—such a government is the worst *despotism* we can think of (a constitution that subverts all the freedom of the subjects, who would have no freedom whatsoever). Not a *paternal* but rather a *patriotic* government (*imperium non paternale, sed patrioticum*) is the only one thinkable for men who are capable of having rights, and the only one thinkable for a benevolent ruler. The *patriotic* mentality [*Denkungsart*] is such that everyone in the nation (the ruler himself not excepted) considers the commonwealth to be the maternal womb or the land to be the paternal soil out of and from which he himself sprang and which he must also therefore leave behind as a treasured pledge. Thus, each considers himself authorized to protect the rights of the commonwealth by laws deriving from the general will, but not authorized to subject it to his own unconditioned, discretionary use. This right of freedom comes to him who is a member of the commonwealth as a human being, insofar as this latter is a being who is in general capable of having rights.

2. I express [the principle of] the *equality* of subjects in the following formula: Every member of the commonwealth has coercive rights in relation to every other member, excepting only its ruler, who has the authority to coerce without himself being subject to any coercive law (for he is not a member of the commonwealth, but its creator or preserver). Everyone in a nation who is *subject to* laws is a subject and consequently is, along with all other members of the commonwealth, subject to the right of coercion; only one individual (physical or moral person), the nation's ruler, through whom all rightful coercion is exercised, is excepted. For if he could be coerced, he would not be the nation's ruler, and the sequence of subordination would ascend infinitely upward. If, however, there were two (persons free from coercion), neither of them would be subject to coercive laws, and neither could treat the other unjustly; and that is impossible.

This complete equality of men as subjects in a nation is completely consistent with the greatest inequality in the quantity and degree of possessions they have, whether these be physical or mental superiority over others, or fortuitously acquired external goods, or, to speak generally, rights (of which there can be many) with respect to others. And, thus, the welfare of one very much depends on the will of another (that of the poor on that of the rich), one must obey (as the child its elder or the wife her husband) while the other commands, and one must serve (as laborer) while the other pays, etc. Nonetheless, as regards *right* (which, as the expression of the general will, can only be

291

292

singular, for it concerns the form of right and not the matter or object regarding which I have rights) they are as subjects all equal to one another. For no one can coerce anyone else except through public law (and its executor, the nation's ruler), but through this everyone else can resist him in the same way; no one can lose this authority to coerce (and to have rights with respect to) others except by breaking the law; and no one can renounce this right, i.e, no one can make a contract or perform some rightful act [*rechtliche Handlung*] whereby he has no rights but only duties, for in so doing he would rob himself of the right to make a contract and would consequently cancel the contract itself.

From this idea of the equality of men as subjects in the commonwealth also comes this formula: Every member of the commonwealth must be permitted to attain any degree of status (to which a subject can aspire) to which his talent, his industry, and his luck may bring him; and his fellow subjects may not block his way by [appealing to] hereditary prerogatives (as the privilege belonging to a particular class) and thereby eternally hinder him and his descendants.

Because all right consists merely in the limitation of the freedom of all others, granted that within the context of universal laws the rights of others can coexist with mine; and because public right (in a commonwealth) is merely the state of an actual legislation that both accords with this principle and is enforced by power—a power through which all who belong to a people exist as subjects in a general state of right [*rechtlichen Zustand*] (*status iuridicus*), that is, in an equilibrium of effect and counter-effect that conforms to universal laws of freedom limiting everyone's will [*Willkür*] (which is called the civil state); it follows that in this state (before a person has performed any act affecting this right) every person has the precisely *identical innate*
293 *right* to coerce others to exercise their freedom within just such bounds as remain compatible with the exercise of one's own freedom. Since birth is not an act of him who is born, it cannot create any inequality regarding the rights pertaining to his state, nor can it subject him to any coercive laws except those he shares in common with all others as subject of the sole supreme legislative power; thus, one member as co-subject of a commonwealth can have no innate privilege [*Vorrecht*] over another. And no person can bequeath to his descendants the privilege of status he has within the commonwealth; nor, consequently, can anyone forcibly prevent them from attaining by virtue of their own merit even higher steps in the hierarchy (where one is *superior,* the other *inferior,* but neither is *imperans,* nor *subiectus*), just as if they were qualified by birth for the status of masters. A person may bequeath everything else as long as it is material (and does not pertain to his person), for it can be acquired and disposed of by him as property, and thus a sequence of generations can bring about considerable inequality in financial circumstances among the members of a commonwealth (between wage earners and employers, and landowners and agricultural workers, etc.). But a person is prevented from hindering others when their talent, industry, and good fortune make it

possible for them to rise to circumstances equal to his. Otherwise a person would have to be able to coerce without being subject to coercive resistance from others, and that goes beyond the status of a fellow-subject. Except through some transgression of his own, no person who lives in the state of right obtaining in a commonwealth can lose this equality, neither through a contract nor through military occupation (*occupatio bellica*); for there is no act (neither his own nor that of another) that conforms with right whereby he can terminate his possession of himself and thus enter into the class of domestic animals, which can be used in any capacity one desires and can be kept in that state without their consent as long as one pleases, even given the restriction (which is sometimes sanctioned by religion, as among the Indians) not to disfigure or kill them.[17] A person's state can be regarded as fortunate if only he is aware that his failure to rise to status equal to that of others is due to himself alone (his abilities or earnestness of will) or to circumstances for which he can blame no one else, and not because of the irresistible will of another. For in regard to rights, a person's fellow-subjects in the commonwealth have no advantage over him.*

294

3. *Independence* (*sibisufficientia*) of a member of the commonwealth as a citizen, i.e., as co-legislator. Regarding the issue of legislation itself, everyone is free and equal under presently existing law, yet not everyone can be considered equal with respect to the right of making these laws. Even so, those who are not capable of having this right are obligated as members of the commonwealth to follow these laws and to share in their protection, but only as *partakers* in it, not as *citizens*. All right depends on laws. However, a public law that determines what will be allowed or forbidden for everyone is the act of a public will, from which all right comes and which must not therefore be able to deny rights to anyone. This is possible [i.e., establishing

---

*If one tries to attach a determinate concept to the term *gracious* (as distinct from "kind," "benevolent," "protective," and so on) one can see that it pertains only to someone who is not subject to any *coercive rights*. Thus, only the head of the *nation's government*, who produces and distributes all benefits that are possible under public laws (for the *sovereign* who gives those laws is, in effect, invisible, and is law itself personified, not its agent) can, as the only one against whom there is no coervice right, be entitled *gracious lord*. Even in an aristocracy, as, e.g., in Venice, the *senate* is the only *gracious lord;* the nobility that constitutes it, not even excepting the Doge (for only the *Grand Council* is sovereign) are subjects and, where the execution of laws is concerned, are equal to everyone else, just because every subject has coercive rights against each of them. Princes (i.e., persons who govern by virtue of heredity) are (through courtly etiquette and courtesy) called gracious lord only in prospect of their future rule and in respect to their claim to it; but as regards their proprietary status, they are still fellow-subjects, against whom their humblest servant must have, through the nation's ruler, a coercive right. Thus there can be no more than one single gracious lord in a nation. As concerns the gracious (more properly esteemed) ladies, they can be regarded as claiming this title by virtue of their rank and sex (and thus they can claim it only from the *male* sex), and only because of the refinement of manners (called gallantry), whereby the male sex believes it does itself the greater honor by conceding precedence to the fairer sex.

public law] through no other will than that belonging to the people collectively (since all decide for all, hence each for himself); for only
295 to oneself can one never deny rights. However, were it any will but this one—since the will of a person cannot make a decision for someone different from himself without denying the latter's rights—it would follow that such a will's laws would require another law limiting its legislation; consequently, no particular will can legislate for the commonwealth. (Strictly speaking, the concept of a commonwealth is constituted from the concepts of the external freedom, the equality of each person's will, and the *unity* of the wills of *all,* and the last of these requires a vote, because the presence of freedom and equality presupposes independence.) This fundamental law that only arises from the general (unified) will of the people [*Volkswille*] is called the *original contract.*

Any person who has the right to vote [*Stimmrecht*] on this legislation is called a *citizen* (*citoyen,* i.e., citizen of the nation, not citizen of a town, *bourgeois*). The only quality necessary for being a citizen, other than the *natural* one (that he is neither a child nor a woman), is that he be *his own master* (*sui iuris*), consequently that he have some *property* to support himself (among which we can count any skill, craft, fine art or science), i.e., in cases where he must acquire the means of life from others, he can do so only by *selling* what is *his** and not by granting others the use of his labor, so that in the proper sense of the word he *serves* no one but the commonwealth. Here, then,
296 craftsmen and large (or small) landowners are all equal, each entitled to one vote. For in regard to land ownership, we may disregard the question as to how someone might rightfully have come to possess more than he can cultivate with his own hands (for acquisition by military conquest is not primary acquisition), and how it occurred that in order to live so many persons who would otherwise have been able to acquire permanent property were thereby reduced to merely serving those landowners. It would conflict with the foregoing principle of equality if a law granted large landowners such privileged status that their descendants would either always remain large (feudal) landowners, without their land being divided by sale or inheritance and thus coming to be used by more people, or even that in the case of

---

*Whoever produces an *opus* can *transfer* it to another by *selling* it, just as if it were his own property. *Praestatio operae* [promising one's labor], however, is not a sale. The domestic servant, the shop clerk, the laborer, or even the barber are merely *operarii* [laborers], not *artifices* [artisans] (in the wider sense of the term), thus not members of the nation, and thus not qualified to be citizens. Although he to whom I give my firewood to chop, and the tailor to whom I give cloth from which to make a suit of clothes, seem to stand in completely similar relationships to me, the former differs from the latter as a barber does from a wig-maker (to whom I may also have given the hair from which to make my wig), and as a laborer from an artist or craftsman, whose completed work belongs to him as long as he has not been paid for it. As tradesman, the latter exchanges his property with others (*opus*), but the laborer permits others to use his labor (*operam*). It is, I admit, somewhat difficult to determine what requirements a person must meet so that he can be his own master.

such division no one but those belonging to a certain arbitrarily designated class of men could acquire part of it. The large landowner eliminates as many smaller landholders and their votes as could otherwise occupy his place; thus, he does not vote in their name and therefore has only one vote. It must be left solely to the ability, earnestness, and luck of each member of the commonwealth that each be able to acquire a part of it and that all be able to acquire it in its entirety, though these distinctions cannot become a matter of universal legislation. The number of those eligible to vote on legislation must be based on the number of those possessing the means of livelihood, not on the quantity of their possessions.

However, *everyone* who has this voting right must agree to this law of public justice [*Gerechtigkeit*]; otherwise, a conflict of rights will arise among those who do not agree to it, and a still higher principle of right will be required to decide the issue. Since unanimity cannot be expected of an entire people, the only attainable outcome that one can foresee is to obtain a majority of the vote, and (in a large population) not even a majority of the direct vote, but only a majority of those delegated as representatives of the people. Thus, we will assume that the principle of allowing this majority to suffice [for legislation] has received universal agreement, that it is a matter of contract, and that it must be the ultimate basis for establishing a civil constitution.

Conclusion 297

Here, then, is an *original contract* among men on which alone a civil constitution can be based, one that is thus completely compatible with right and by means of which a commonwealth can be established. But it is by no means assumed as a *fact* (and, indeed, it is utterly impossible) that this contract effects a coalition of every particular and private will within a people so as to form a common and public will (for the sake of legislating in accord with right); nor must it first be shown historically that a people, whose rights and obligations we as their descendants assume, must once have actually carried out such an act and must have left us an authentic report or instrument of it, either orally or in writing, before we can regard ourselves as bound by an already existing civil constitution. Instead, it is a *mere idea* of reason, one, however, that has indubitable (practical) reality.[18] Specifically, it obligates every legislator to formulate his laws in such a way that they *could* have sprung from the unified will of the entire people and to regard every subject, insofar as he desires to be a citizen, as if he had joined in voting for such a will. For that is the criterion of every public law's conformity with right. If a public law is so formulated that an entire people *could not possibly* agree to it (as, e.g., that a particular class of *subjects* has the hereditary privilege of being a *ruling class*), it is not just; however, if *only* it is *possible* that a people could agree to it, it is a duty to regard that law as just, even if the people are presently in such a position or disposition of mind [*Denkungsart*] that if asked it would probably withhold its consent.*

However, this restriction obviously applies only to the judgment of legislators, not to that of the subject. Thus, if a people should judge that a particular actual [piece of] legislation would in all probability cause them to forfeit their happiness, what should they do about it? Should they not resist it? There can be only one answer: nothing can be done about it, except to obey. For the point at issue here is not the happiness that a subject can expect to derive from the establishment and administration of the commonwealth; instead, the foremost issue is the rights that are thereby secured for everyone, which is the supreme principle, limited by no other, from which all maxims concerning the commonwealth must be derived. In regard to the first issue (happiness), no universally valid principles can be laid down as laws. For both the temporal circumstances and the deeply conflicting and thus continually changing illusions in which each person places his happiness (though no one can prescribe for another where he should place it) make all fixed principles impossible, and happiness is in itself unfit as a principle underlying legislation. The proposition *salus publica suprema civitatis lex est*[19] remains undiminished in value and esteem; but the [aspect of the] public's well-being to receive *first* consideration is precisely that legal contract securing everyone's freedom through laws, that contract whereby each person remains at liberty to seek his happiness in any way he thinks best so long as he does not violate that universal freedom under law and, consequently, the rights of other fellow subjects.

If the supreme power makes laws directed primarily towards happiness (the prosperity of citizens, increasing population, and so on), this does not happen because it is the purpose of establishing a civil constitution. Instead, it is merely a means for *securing* the *state of right,* especially against the people's external enemies. The nation's leader must be authorized to be the sole judge as to whether such laws are in the interest of the commonwealth's prosperity, which is necessary to secure its strength and stability against both internal and external enemies. The purpose is not, as it were, to make the people happy against their will, but only to make them exist as a commonwealth.† Now the legislator can indeed err in his judgment about

*If, for example, a proportional war tax were imposed on all subjects, they could not, because it was oppressive or perhaps because in their opinion the war was unnecessary, call it unjust for they are not entitled [*nicht berechtigt*] to judge in such matters, because it always remains *possible* that the war is unavoidable and the tax indispensable, in which case the subjects must judge the tax to be right. But if certain landowners were beset by the burdens of such a war, while others of the same class were exempted, one can easily see that an entire people could not agree to such a law, and it is at least entitled to make representations against it, since the people can never regard this unequal distribution of burdens as just.

† Certain import restrictions might be included among such measures, restrictions

whether or not these measures are *prudent,* but he cannot err when he asks himself whether or not the law agrees with the principle of right. For in the idea of the original contract he actually has in hand an infallible standard [of right], one that is, indeed, *a priori* (and he need not wait for experience to teach him whether the means are suitable, as would be necessary were he to adopt the principle of happiness). Only if it is not contradictory to believe that an entire people can agree to such a law is it compatible with right, however much pain it may bring. Now if a public law can receive such agreement, it follows that it is irreproachable (*irreprehensibel*) in relation to the right and thus carries with it the authority to coerce and, at the same time, the prohibition against actively resisting the will of the legislator. That is, the power of the nation that makes law effective is also unopposable (*irresistibel*), and there is no rightfully constituted commonwealth without the power to put down all internal resistance, for such resistance would have to derive from a maxim that, if made universal, would destroy all civil constitutions, thus annihilating the only state in which men can possess rights.

From this it follows that all resistance to the supreme legislative power, all incitement of subjects actively to express discontent, all revolt that breaks forth into rebellion, is the highest and most punishable crime in a commonwealth, for it destroys its foundation.[20] And this prohibition is *absolute,* so that even if that power or its agent, the nation's leader, may have broken the original contract, thereby forfeiting in the subject's eyes the right to be legislator, since he has authorized the government to proceed in a thoroughly brutal (tyrannical) fashion, the citizen is nonetheless not to resist him in any way whatsoever. This is because under an already existing civil constitution the people no longer have the right to judge and to determine how the constitution should be administered. For suppose they had such a right and, indeed, that they opposed the actual judgment of the nation's leader, then who would determine on which side the right lies? Neither of them can serve as judge in his own case. Thus, there would have to be still another head above the head to decide between the latter and the people—and that is contradictory. Nor, for instance, can one invoke a right of necessity here [*Nothrecht*] (*ius in casu necessitatis*)—that is, a purported *right* to violate the right under supreme (physical) *duress,* which is an absurdity anyway*—so as to

300

---

that might promote the subjects' means of livelihood in their own best interest, rather than to the advantage of foreigners or to the stimulation of foreign industry; for unless the people are prosperous, the nation will not possess strength sufficient to resist external enemies or to maintain itself as a commonwealth.

*There is no *Casus necessitatis,* except where duties, to wit, *absolute* duties and (indeed perhaps major but nonetheless) *conditional* duties, conflict with one another. For example, to prevent some misfortune from befalling the nation, one person might have to betray another to whom he was related, perhaps a father and son. This prevention of evil to the nation is an absolute duty, while preventing the latter from succumbing to

provide a means of raising the barrier that limits the people's power. For the head of the nation can as easily justify his harsh treatment of the subjects by appeal to their rebelliousness as they can justify their unrest by adducing complaints about unwarranted suffering at his hands. And who will decide the issue? Only he who is the supreme arbiter of public right can do so—and that is precisely the nation's leader. Thus no one in the commonwealth can have a right to challenge that authority.

301   Nonetheless I find respectable men do advocate this authority of subjects to oppose their superiors in certain circumstances. Among these I will here cite only *Achenwall*,[21] who is very cautious, precise, and restrained in his doctrines of natural right.* He says: "If the danger that threatens the commonwealth from enduring the leader's injustice any longer is greater than the danger to be feared from taking up arms against him, then the people may resist him, may on the basis of this right set aside their contract of subjection, and may dethrone him as a tyrant." And he concludes: "In this way (in relation to their former ruler) the people return to the state of nature."

I can easily believe that neither *Achenwall* nor any of the other worthy men who have reasoned along similar lines would ever in an actual case have given their counsel and agreement to such serious undertakings. And it can hardly be doubted that had the uprisings by which Switzerland, the United Netherlands or even Great Britain won their much vaunted constitutions failed, the readers of their histories would regard the execution of the now celebrated authors of those constitutions as well-deserved punishment of persons guilty of high treason. For the outcome of an act commonly influences our judgment about its rightness, even though the former was uncertain, while the latter is certain. But in matters of right, it is clear that people who seek to secure their rights in this way perpetrate a wrong [*Unrecht*] of the highest degree—even where one grants that no wrong [*Unrecht*] is done to a prince (who had violated, say, a *joyeuse entrée*, or an actual basic contract with the people) by such an uprising. For (if made a maxim) the latter would render all just constitutions insecure and

---

misfortune is only a conditional duty (specifically, it is conditional upon his having not committed a crime against the nation). The first person might report the second's plans to the authorities, though with the greatest unwillingness; yet (moral) necessity compels him to do so. However, if in order to save his own life one shipwrecked person who shoved another away from the board he is holding onto were to say that he had done so from (physical) necessity, his claim would be completely false. For the preservation of my life is only a conditional duty (conditional on my being able to do so without committing a crime); but the duty not to take the life of another who has not injured me or who has not endangered me with the loss of my own life is unconditional. Yet teachers of universal civil right justifiably authorize such measures as are required in emergencies. For the authorities cannot attach any *punishment* to the prohibition since that punishment would have to be death. It would have to be an absurd law that threatened anyone with death if he did not freely give in to death in dangerous circumstances.

*Ius Naturae. Editio quinta. Pars posterior, §§ 203-206.

would introduce a state of complete lawlessness, where at the least all right would lose its sanction. Regarding this tendency of so many well-intentioned authors to plead on behalf of the people (and to its own detriment), I will only note that in discussions of right its source is the common fallacy of substituting the principle of happiness for the principle of right. But it is also partly because no actual contract, submitted by the commonwealth, accepted by its head, and sanctioned by both, can be found. And such authors assume that some event [corresponding] to the idea of that original contract, whose basis lies in reason, must *actually* have occurred. Thus, they believe that in its absence the people retain the authority to depart at its discretion from the contract whenever in its own judgment there is a violation of it.* 302

Here, obviously, the principle of happiness (which is, in fact, not capable of clear formulation) has as evil an effect in regard to political right as it does in morals, despite the best intentions of those who teach it. The sovereign wants to make the people happy in accord with his own concept of happiness and becomes a despot; the people will not give up their universal human claim to their own happiness and become rebels. Had one first asked what is right (regarding which the *a priori* principles remain fixed and cannot be botched by the empiricist) the idea of the social contract would retain its unassailable authority, though not as a fact (as Danton,[22] would have it, declaring that with the lack of such a fact all existing rights and all property under actually existing constitutions are null and void), but as a rational principle for judging any rightful [*rechtlichen*] public constitution whatsoever. And one would then see that, before there is a general will, the people possess no coercive right against their ruler, since the right to coerce can be exercised only through him. But even if the general will does exist, the people cannot coerce the ruler, because then they themselves would be the supreme ruler. Consequently, the people never have the right of coercion (neither in word nor in deed) over the nation's leader.

We can also see that practice amply confirms this theory. In Great 303 Britain, where the people make such a to-do over their constitution that they seem to hold it up as a model for the entire world, we nonetheless find the constitution completely silent regarding the people's authority in case the monarch were to transgress the constitution

---

*No matter how the actual contract between the people and their leader might be broken, the people cannot immediately react as a commonwealth but only as a mob. For the previously existing constitution has been torn up by the people, and their organization into a new commonwealth has yet to occur. At this point the state of anarchy with all its at least possible terrors arises, and the wrong that happens in this situation is, therefore, that which each faction of the people does to every other, which is made clear by the foregoing example, where the rebellious subjects of that nation finally wanted to use force to impose a much more oppressive constitution than the one they overthrew. That is, they would have been devoured by clerics and aristocrats, rather than have been able to expect an all-governing leader to distribute the nation's burdens more equitably.

of 1688; consequently, since no law covers this case, if he violated the contract, the people tacitly reserve the right to rebel against him. It would be an obvious contradiction for the constitution to include a law governing this case, giving the people the right to overthrow the existing constitution, from which all specific laws derive (even laws covering breach of contract), for it would then necessarily contain a *publicly constituted** opposing power, thus a second head of the nation to protect the people's rights against the first one, in consequence of which there would also have to be a third to decide with whom the right lies as between the other two heads. Carefully guarding against such accusations in the event their undertaking should fail, those guides (or guardians, if you will) of the [British] people who frightened the monarch off, preferred to *attribute* to him a voluntary surrender of sovereignty than to claim for themselves the right to dethrone him, whereby the constitution would clearly have been rendered self-contradictory.

Now since no one, I trust, will accuse me of flattering the monarchs too much by maintaining their inviolability, I also hope to be spared the accusation of favoring the people too much when I say that they likewise have inalienable rights in respect of the nation's ruler, even though these cannot be coercive rights.

Hobbes is of the opposite opinion. According to him (*de Cive*, Chap. 7, sec. 14)[24] the nation's ruler is not contractually obligated to the people and cannot wrong the citizens (no matter how he might dispose of them.)—This proposition would be entirely correct, if by "wrong" [*Unrecht*] one understood an injury [*Läsion*][25] that gave the injured party a *coercive right* against the one who had wronged him; but stated so generally, the proposition is terrifying.

The cooperative subject must be able to assume that his ruler does not want to wrong him. Consequently on this assumption—because every man has inalienable rights that he cannot give up even if he wanted to and in regard to which he has the authority to be his own judge—the wrong that in his view befalls him occurs only as a function of error, or from ignorance of certain of the consequences of the supreme power's laws. Thus, regarding whatever in the ruler's decrees seem to wrong the commonwealth, the citizen must retain the authority to make his opinions publicly known, and this authority must receive the ruler's approval. For to assume that the ruler cannot ever err or that he cannot be ignorant of something would be to portray him as blessed with divine inspiration and as elevated above the rest of humanity. Hence *freedom of the pen*—within the bounds of respect and love for the constitution one lives under, respect and love that are

304

---

*No right in a nation can be tacitly, and thus silently and treacherously, reserved, least of all the right by which the people claim to come under the constitution; for all laws by which the people are governed must be thought of as springing from a public will. Thus, if the constitution allowed rebellion, it would have to declare this right publicly and explain how it might be exercised.[23]

maintained by the subjects' liberal manner of thought [*Denkungsart*], a way of thinking instilled in them by that very constitution (and to which way of thinking the pens restrict one another so as not to lose their freedom)—is the sole protector of the people's rights. To want to deprive citizens of this right is not only tantamount to depriving them of all claim to rights in relation to the supreme commander (according to Hobbes), but it also denies to him, whose will commands subjects as citizens only because it represents the general will of the people, all knowledge of such matters as he would himself change if he knew about them; and denying such freedom places the commander in a self-contradictory position. Encouraging the leader to suspect that unrest might be aroused by men thinking out loud and for themselves is to awaken in him both distrust in his own power and hate for his people.[26]

The general principle by which a people may judge, though merely negatively, as to whether the supreme legislature has *not decreed* with the best of intentions is contained in this proposition: *Whatever a people cannot decree for itself cannot be decreed for it by the legislator.*[27]

If, for example, the question is whether one can view a certain previously instituted ecclesiastical constitution as expressing the permanently enduring actual will (and intent) of the legislator, one would have first to ask whether a people *may* enact for itself a law [specifying] that, once adopted, certain articles of faith and religious practices should endure forever, and thus whether it may prevent itself in the person of its descendants from further advancement in religious insight or from eventually correcting old errors? It will now be clear that an original contract among the people that made this a law would be in and of itself null and void, for it would conflict with humanity's vocation and end. Consequently, a law enacted to this end cannot be the monarch's true will, and one can therefore offer him counterarguments against it. In all cases, however, when something of this sort is thus decreed by the supreme legislator, it is subject to general and public judgment, but resistance to it in word or deed must never be mustered.

305

Within the mechanism of the nation's constitution, there must in every commonwealth be an *obedience* to coercive laws (that apply to all), but at the same time, there must also be a *spirit of freedom,* for in matters of universal human duty everyone desires, in order not to be placed in a self-contradictory position, to be convinced rationally that this coercion accords with right. Obedience without the spirit of freedom is the proximate cause of all *secret societies.* For mankind is called by nature to communicate among itself, especially in matters of general concern to men, and those societies would disappear if this freedom were encouraged. And how else can the government come by the knowledge that so particularly concerns its own essential intention than by allowing the spirit of freedom, so worthy of respect in its origin and effects, to express itself.

*   *
*

Nowhere will a practice that foregoes all pure principles of reason more arrogantly deny theory than with respect to the question of what the requirements of a good national constitution are. The reason for this is that a longstanding lawful constitution gradually accustoms the people to make it their rule to judge both their happiness and their rights on the basis of that previous state of affairs in which everything has proceeded calmly; conversely, they are not accustomed to evaluat-
306   ing that state of affairs on the basis of the concepts of happiness and right with which reason supplies them; instead, they always prefer the passive state to the dangerous position of seeking a better one (a position in which what Hippocrates told physicians to take to heart holds, *iudicum anceps, experimentum periculosum*).[28] Now since all constitutions that have endured for a sufficiently long time, their inadequacies and differences be what they may, yield uniform results, namely, satisfaction with the state one is in, it follows that when one looks to the *people's welfare,* everything depends not in the least on theory, but only on practice that derives from experience.

But if there is in reason something that can be expressed by the term *political right,* and if in this concept men, who because of their freedom stand in antagonistic relations to one another, are still able to find a unifying force and, consequently, objective (practical) reality, regardless of the good or evil that may originate in it (which evils can be known only through experience), this concept is grounded in *a priori* principles (for what is right can never be taught by experience), and there is a *theory* of political right. Any practice that does not conform to it lacks all legitimacy.

Now to this no exception can be taken except that, although men have in their heads some idea of the rights due them, they are, by virtue of their hardheartedness, incapable and unworthy of being treated accordingly; and, therefore, a supreme power who uses only pruden-tial rules may and must keep them in order. This desperate step (*salto mortale*) is of such a nature that when once the issue becomes one of might, not of right, the people may also seek their own power and thus render all lawful constitutions insecure. If there is nothing that im-mediately commands rational respect (such as the rights of men), all influences on men's wills [*Willkür*] are incapable of restraining their freedom. But when in addition to benevolence the right speaks out loudly, then human nature will not show itself so debased as not to listen reverently to its voice. (*Tum pietate gravem meritisque si forte virum quem Conspexere, silent arrectisque auribus adstant.* Vergil.)[29]

On the Relationship of Theory to Practice
in International Right, Considered
from a Universally Philanthropic,
i.e., Cosmopolitan Point of View.*

(Against Moses Mendelssohn)

Is the human race as a whole to be loved; or is it something that one is to view with distaste, wishing it all the best (so as not to become misanthropic), but not really expecting it, so that we turn our attention away from it, though with feelings of regret? The answer to this question depends on the answer we give to another: Do mankind's natural tendencies allow us to infer that the race will always progress toward the better and that the evil of present and past times will in the future disappear? For if this were so, we could at least love the race for its constant approach to the good; otherwise, we must either hate or despise it, the contrary blandishments of those possessing a general love of mankind (which love would consist at most of benevolent love, not complaisant love) be what they may. For we cannot avoid hating in human nature—even when we try most strongly to love it—what is and will remain evil, especially the deliberate and mutual violation of man's most sacred rights. We may not actually want to do men harm because of this evil, yet we do want as little to do with them as possible.

Moses Mendelssohn was of the latter opinion (*Jerusalem,* second section, pp. 44–47),[30] an opinion he opposed to his friend *Lessing's* hypothesis of a divine education of the human race. To him it is a fantasy, "that the whole of humanity here below should in the course of time always move forward and perfect itself. We see," says he, "that the human race as a whole swings slowly back and forth, and it never takes a few steps forward without soon afterward relapsing twice as fast into its previous state." (This is just the Sisyphean boulder; and with it one assumes, as the Hindus do, that the Earth is a place for   308 repenting of old and no longer remembered sins.) "The individual man progresses; but humanity constantly vacillates between fixed limits; considered as whole, however, humanity maintains during all periods of time about the same level of morality, the same degree of religion and irreligion, of virtue and vice, of happiness (?)[31] and of misery." He introduces these contentions (p. 46) by saying, "Do you want to guess what Providence's intentions for mankind are? Forge no hypotheses (earlier he had called these theories); look only at what actually happens, and, if you can, take a glance at the history of all

*It is not immediately apparent how a universally *philanthropic* presupposition points to a *cosmopolitan* constitution, nor how the latter indicates a foundation in *international right* as the sole state in which the human tendencies that make our species lovable can be developed. The conclusion of this section will make these connections clear.

ages and look at what has previously happened. This is fact; this must have been among those intentions, must have been approved within wisdom's plans, or at least been adopted along with them.''

I am of another opinion. If seeing a virtuous man struggling with tribulations and temptations towards evil and yet holding his own against them is a sight fit for a divinity, so is it a most unfit sight for even the commonest but well intentioned man, not to mention a divinity, to see the human race advancing from period to period towards virtue and then soon afterwards to see it again falling as deeply back into vice and misery as it was before. Observing this tragedy for a while may perhaps be moving and instructive, but the curtain must finally fall. For in the long run it becomes a farce; and if the actors do not become weary of it, since they are fools, the spectator will when, after one or another act, he has sufficient grounds for assuming that the never ending piece will be eternally the same. To be sure, if it is only a play, the punishment that comes at the end can make up for the unpleasant sensations experienced along the way. But allowing vice to mount upon endless vice in the real world (even with an occasional virtuous act interjected) so that in days to come there can be plenty to punish is, to say the least, contrary to our conception of the morality of a wise creator and governor of the world.[32]

309   I will thus permit myself to assume that since the human race's natural end is to make steady cultural progress, its moral end is to be conceived as progressing toward the better. And this progress may well be occasionally *interrupted,* but it will never be *broken off.* It is not necessary for me to prove this assumption; the burden of proof is on its opponents. For I rest my case on my innate duty—a duty belonging to everyone in the sequence of generations to which (as man in general) I belong, though as regards the moral character required of me I am not as good as I ought to or can be—the duty so to affect posterity that it will become continually better (something that must be assumed to be possible). And this duty can rightfully be passed on from one generation to another. Now history may well give rise to so many doubts concerning my hopes that, were they demonstrable, they could move me to give up an apparently futile task; yet as long as this futility cannot be shown to be completely certain, I cannot exchange my duty (the *liquidum*) for the rule of expediency not to undertake the unattainable (the *illiquidum,* since it is merely hypothetical). And however uncertain I may always be, and may remain, as to whether we may hope anything better for the human race, yet this uncertainty can detract neither from the maxim that from a practical point of view it is attainable, nor from the presupposition of its necessity.

This hope for better times, without which an earnest desire to do something that benefits the general good would never have warmed the human heart, has always influenced the work of the well-intentioned; and good Mendelssohn must have counted on it when he so eagerly strove for the enlightenment and welfare of the nation to which he belonged. Because unless others after him continued further down the same path, he could not by himself, alone, rationally hope to bring them about. Faced with the sorry sight not so much of the evil to which the human race is subjected by natural causes, but rather of those that men themselves inflict on one another, the mind is nonetheless cheered by the prospect of a better future. This attitude is quite disinterestedly benevolent, for we shall long be in the grave and shall not harvest the fruit we have helped to sow. Empirical arguments against the success of these resolutions, which are based on hope, fail here. For the argument that something has until now been unsuccessful and therefore shall never be successful does not justify abandoning even a pragmatic or technical intention (for example, travel by aerostatic balloons), much less a morally obligatory one, unless, of course, its attainment is demonstrably impossible. Besides, one can offer a great deal of evidence showing that the human race as a whole has in our age, by comparison with all earlier ones, bettered itself morally and to a considerable degree (and short-lived checks to such betterment prove nothing to the contrary). One can also offer evidence showing that the cry over the irresistible growth in human depravity is due to the fact that, when man attains a higher stage of morality, one can see further still and can make more rigorous judgments regarding what man is in comparison with what he ought to be; consequently, our self-censure will always be the more rigorous the more stages of morality have been ascended in the known course of the world.

If we now inquire as to the means by which this eternal progress towards betterment can be maintained and perhaps even sped up, one soon sees that this immeasurably distant result depends not so much on what *we* do (e.g. on the education we give the world's children), nor on what method we adopt so as to bring it about; instead, it depends on what human *nature does in and with us so as to compel us onto a path that we ourselves would not readily follow*. Only from nature, or rather only from *providence* (since supreme wisdom is required for the fulfillment of this end), can we anticipate a result that will affect the whole and, as a consequence, the parts. For, by contrast, human plans begin only with the parts, even if they do not stop there; and while men's ideas [*Ideen*] can extend to the whole as such, their influence cannot, not just because it is too vast for them, but primarily because it would be difficult for them to freely unify their conflicting plans into a single purpose.[33]

Just as universal violence and its resultant duress must ultimately bring a people to the point of deciding to submit to the coercion of public laws—a coercion that reason itself prescribes to them—and to enter into a civil constitution, so also must the duress of constant wars, in which nations in their turn seek to reduce or subjugate one another, at last bring them to the point of entering into a cosmopolitan constitution, even against their wills. Or, if such a state of

310

311   universal freedom is for its part even more dangerous (as in outsized nations it has indeed more than once been) because it leads to the most terrifying despotism, this duress must compel nations to that state in which, while there is no cosmopolitan commonwealth under a single head, there is nonetheless a rightful state of federation that conforms to commonly accepted [principles of] *international right.*

For since the advancing culture of nations—along with their simultaneously increasing tendency to aggrandize themselves by guile or force at the cost of others—will multiply the number of wars, and since there will, because of that, be ever swelling standing armies (paid at the same rate) to keep in training and to equip with increasingly numerous instruments of war, expenditures must continuously increase. Meanwhile, the price of all necessities constantly grows, even without hope for a proportionately expanding growth in representative metal currencies. No peace endures long enough for the savings accumulated during it to equal the next war's expenditures; and against this the invention of national debt is an ingenious but ultimately self-defeating expedient. Thus, impotence must finally bring about what good will ought to have done, but did not: Every nation must be so organized internally that not the head of the nation—for whom, properly speaking, war has no cost (since he puts the expense off on others, namely the people)—but rather the people who pay for it have the decisive voice as to whether or not there should be war. (Of course, this necessarily presupposes the realization of the idea of that original contract.) For only hesitantly will the people place itself in danger of personal penury—a penury that never threatens the nation's head—out of lust for self-aggrandizement, or over a purported and merely verbal affront. Thus, succeeding generations (unburdened by debts they themselves have not incurred) will be able even in a moral sense to make ever more progress towards bettering themselves. And they will do this not as a result of any love of their ancestors for them, but rather solely by virtue of their ancestors' self-love. Since every commonwealth unable to harm others by force must rely only on the right, it can reasonably hope to receive help in doing so from other similarly constituted commonwealths.

Meanwhile, this is only opinion and mere hypothesis—as uncertain
312   as all judgments claiming to set out the sole appropriate natural cause for an intended effect that is not entirely in our power. And even as such it does not contain (as was previously shown) a principle whereby subjects in an already existing nation may enforce its adoption; instead, only uncoercible leaders may do this. Although in the normal course of events it is not human nature to relinquish power voluntarily, by the same token under pressing circumstances it is nonetheless not impossible for it to do so. Thus, one of the not inadequate expressions of the wishes and hopes of men (conscious of their own inability) is to expect the required circumstances from *providence*—a providence that brings the end of the *humanity* as a whole to a successful

issue, the fulfillment of mankind's ultimate vocation through the free use of its limited powers, an end that the *ends of men,* taken separately, directly oppose. For even the opposition of inclinations, from which springs all evil, gives reason free play to subjugate all men and to give reign to the good, which when once it exists furthers and sustains itself, rather than to evil, which is self-destructive.

*   *

*

Human nature never seems less lovable than in the relations among entire peoples. No nation's independence or possessions are even momentarily safe from others. The will to subjugate or to curtail the growth of others is always present, and the preparation for defense that often makes peace more oppressive and destructive of internal welfare than even war can never be relaxed. Now the sole possible remedy for this is a [state] of international right (analogous to the civil or national rights of individual men) based on public laws backed by force and submitted to by every nation. For an enduring universal peace brought about by a so-called *balance of power in Europe* is a mere figment of imagination, like *Swift's house,* whose architect built it so perfectly in accord with all the laws of equilibrium that as soon as a sparrow lit on it, it fell in. But it will be said that nations will never subject themselves to such coercive laws; and the proposal for a universal cosmopolitan nation, to whose power all individual nations 313 should voluntarily submit, and whose laws they should obey, may sound ever so nice in the theory of the Abbe St. Pierre or of a Rousseau, yet it is of no practical use. For this proposal has always been ridiculed by great statesmen, and even more by leaders of nations, as a pedantically childish academic idea.

For my own part, I place my trust in the theory about what the relation among men and nations *ought to be* that derives from the principle of right and that recommends to the earthly gods the maxim always so to proceed in their conflicts that such a universal cosmopolitan nation will thereby be introduced, and thus to assume that it is possible (*in praxi*) and that it *can exist.* At the same time I also trust (*in subsidium*) in the nature of things to compel man to go where he would prefer not to (*fata volentem ducunt, volentem trahunt*).[34] In this latter I also take into account human nature, which, since respect for right and duty remains alive in it, I cannot regard as so immersed in evil that after many unsuccessful attempts, morally practical reason will finally triumph and show it to be lovable. Thus, even on the cosmopolitan level I stand by my assertion: What on rational grounds is true in theory is also useful in practice.

Notes for
Theory and Practice

References to essays in this volume are to page numbers in the *margins.*

1. A. A. VIII, 273–313. This essay first appeared in the *Berlinische Monatsschrift,* September, 1793; the most immediate stimulus to write Theory and Practice seems to have been Kant's reading of Christian Garve's book, *Versuche über verschiedene Gegenstände aus der Moral, der Litteratur und dem gesellschaftlichen Leben,* I, 1792 (*Essays on Various Topics from Morals, Literature, and Social Life*), in which Garve raised a number of objections to Kant's moral theory.

2. See *Crit. Judgment,* xxv–xxviii, 346–7 and B 171/A 132 – B 175/A 136.

3. Apparently a reference to Edmund Burke's *Reflections on the French Revolution* (1790), which had been translated into German in 1792 by Friedrich Gentz.

4. See *Groundings,* 399–400.

5. See *Crit. Prac. Reason,* 108–9.

6. See *Groundings,* 400, 403, 425, 434, 439 and *Crit. Prac. Reason,* 35–41.

7. See *Groundings,* 402n. and *Crit. Prac. Reason,* 78–82.

8. A matter of mere opportunity.

9. See *End of All Things,* 329–30.

10. See *Crit. Prac. Reason,* 22–26, 110–119 and *Met. Prin. Virtue,* 377–8.

11. See *End of All Things,* 334 and A 543/B 571 – A 548/B 576.

12. Christian Garve, *Philosophische Anmerkungen und Abhandlungen zu Ciceros Büchern von den Pflichten* (*Philosophical Notes and Articles on Cicero's Book on Duties*), Breslau, 1783.

13. See *End of All Things,* 336 f. and *Crit. Prac. Reason,* 129–132.

14. I have translated the German term *Staat* by the English term "nation," even though "state" seems initially more natural. My decision is based on three considerations. First, what we think of as a nation, a large

number of people governed under a common constitution, in fact more closely corresponds to Kant's use of *Staat,* than does the present common usage of "state," particularly in this country. Second, Kant uses *Zustand* when he refers to the state of nature and the law-governed state. Here using "state" to translate *Zustand* better conforms with the tradition of English usage going back to Hobbes, than would the more normal rendering of *Zustand* as "condition." Finally, using "state" to render both *Staat* and *Zustand* would have resulted in undesirable confusions. One further note in this regard: I have translated *Volk* quite simply as "people," but readers should be aware that by this term Kant means that state of men created by a social contract (*Vertrag*), by virtue of which they leave the state of nature, but antecedent to the institution of a constitution (*Verfassung*), through which they become a nation (*Staat*). See *Perpetual Peace,* pp. 352, 354.

15. See Kant's letter to Heinrich Jung-Stilling, *Correspondence,* 131–32.

16. Compare *Perpetual Peace,* 349 ff.

17. See *Spec. Beg. Human History,* 114 ff.

18. The phrase *"mere idea* of reason" is for Kant a term of art, denoting a "necessary concept of reason to which no corresponding object can be given in sense experience." A 327/B383 – A 328/B 384, which see.

19. The public well-being is the highest law of the people. See *Perpetual Peace,* 333.

20. See *Met. Elements of Justice,* 318–323.

21. Gottfried Achenwall, *Ius naturae usum auditorem,* Göttingen, 1755–6. Kant used Achenwall's book for his lectures on natural law.

22. Georges Jacques Danton (1759–94), a leader of the French Revolution. That Danton made this or some similar claim cannot be verified.

23. See *Perpetual Peace,* 333.

24. Thomas Hobbes, *De Cive,* ed. Howard Warrender, (Oxford: The Clarendon Press, 1982), Ch. 7, sec. 14. Kant is undoubtedly referring to the original Latin version of this work.

25. Kant's point here seems to be that if by "wrong" Hobbes means physical injury, his view can be accepted; but if it includes violation of rights, it must certainly be incorrect.

26. See *Enlightenment,* 36 ff.

27. See *Perpetual Peace,* 386 f.

28. Judgment is difficult and experiment is dangerous.

29. "If by chance they lay eyes on a man of solid repute/ And prestige, they fall silent and stand with their ears pricked up . . ." Vergil, *Aenied* I, 151–152. (Lind translation.)

30. Moses Mendelssohn, *Jerusalem, oder über religiöse Macht und Judentum (Jerusalem, or On Religious Power and Judaism),* Berlin, 1783. Mendelssohn was among the most important contributors to the Enlightenment movement in Germany, if not all of Europe.

31. Kant's interpolation.

32. See *Universal History,* 18 f., *Spec. Beg. Human History,* 116 f., and *End of All Things,* 330 f.

33. See *Universal History,* 17, *End of All Things,* 337, and *Perpetual Peace,* 365.

34. "Fate guides the willing and drags the unwilling." Seneca, Epistle 107.

The End of All Things[1]
(1794)

It is a common expression, especially when speaking piously, for a dying man to say that he is *passing from time into eternity*.

In fact, this expression would mean nothing if by "eternity" one were to understand the infinite passage of time; for then man would surely never emerge from time, but would always only pass from one moment of time to another. Thus, by this expression must be meant the *end of all time* in man's uninterrupted survival, though we nonetheless mean by this duration (of his existence considered as a quantity) a quantity (*duratio noumenon*) that is utterly incomparable to time, and we surely cannot have any (but a merely negative) concept of it. This thought contains something a bit horrifying, for it leads to an abyss, from which there is no possible return for whosoever falls into it. ("With strong arms Eternity/holds fast in that stern place/him who leaves nothing behind." Haller[2]); yet it also contains something appealing, for one cannot cease from returning one's frightened eyes to it (*nequeunt expleri corda tuendo*. Vergil[3]). It is frightfully-*sublime,* in part because of its obscurity, by which the imagination is made more powerfully active than by bright light. Finally, it must be interwoven into universal human reason in a wonderful way, for it is found in one guise or another among all reasoning peoples in all times. Now since we follow this passage out of time into eternity (whether this idea has objective reality or not), it may, from a theoretical point of view, be considered to extend cognitive knowledge in a moral context, just as when reason itself makes this passage, we come up against the *end of all things* as a [form of] temporal being and as an object of possible experience; however, in the moral order of purposes, this end is at the same time the beginning of the *supersensuous* survival of these same temporal beings, consequently the beginning of their existence as beings that do not stand under conditions of time, and thus their beginning as beings whose state is such as to allow nothing other than a moral evaluation [*Bestimmung*] of their nature.

Days are, as it were, the children of time, since the day that follows, along with all it contains, is the product of the foregoing one. Just as the last child of its parents is called the youngest child, so our language [the German language] has chosen to call the last day (the point in time that concludes all time) the *youngest day*.[4] The youngest day thus still belongs to time; for something happens in it (it does not belong to eternity where nothing more happens, for that would entail passage of time), namely the settling of the accounts of men for their conduct during their entire lifetimes. It is a *judgment day;* the judgment of forgiveness or damnation by the judge of the world is thus the true end of all things in time and, at the same time, the beginning of (a blessed or damned) eternity, in which the fate [*Loos*] that befalls each person remains as it is given to him at the moment in which it (the sentence) is pronounced. Thus the youngest day also includes at the same time the *youngest judgment*. If we should now still count among the *last things* the end of the world as it appears in its present form—namely, the falling of the stars from heaven's vault, the caving in of heaven itself (or its disappearance like a scroll that is rolled up),[5] the burning of both, the creation of a new heaven and a new earth as the place of the blessed and of hell as the one for the damned—that judgment would surely not be the youngest day; for there would still be other, different days to follow it. But since the idea of an end of all things does not have its origin in reasoning about the *physical* world, but is occasioned only by reasoning about the moral course of things in the world; and since the notion of a moral course of things in the world can be ascribed only to the supersensuous (which is understandable only in a moral context)—and the same is true of the idea of eternity; the representation of those last things that come *after* the youngest day can be regarded as a [symbolic] sensuous representation of that final day, along with its moral, though to us not theoretically conceivable, consequences.[6]

However, it is to be noted that from the most ancient times there have been two systems concerning the future eternity: one of them is the *monistic* view of eternity, which grants all men (who are purified by a longer or shorter penance) eternal blessedness; the other is the *dualistic** view, in which *some* are chosen for blessedness, but all *others* are condemned to eternal damnation. For a system in which all were determined to be damned could probably not be defended, since there would be no adequate reason to justify why in general persons had been created; further, the *annihilation* of everyone would indicate a flawed intelligence, who, displeased with his own work, knew of no other means to remedy its shortcomings than to destroy it. In this regard, the dualist faces just the same difficulty that stands in everyone's way when thinking about eternal damnation; for, one could ask, why were the few, indeed, why was only a single person, created if their only reason for being were to be lost for eternity, which is even worse than simply not to exist?[8]

329

*In the ancient Persian religion (of Zoroaster), such a system was based on the hypothesis of two original beings who were locked in eternal battle with one another, the good principle, *Ormuzd,* and the evil one, *Ahriman*. It is extraordinary that the language of two countries that are distant from one another and still more distant from the place where the German language is now spoken is, in the names of these two original beings, German. I remember having read in *Sonnerat* that in *Ava* (the land of the Burmese) the good principle was named *Godeman* (which word also appears to occur in the name *Darius Codomannus*); and since the word Ahriman sounds very similar to *arrant man* [*arge Mann*], present-day Persian also contains a number of original German words. Thus, it may be a task for the scholar of antiquity also to retrace the guiding thread of relations among languages to the origins of many peoples' present *religious* concepts. (See Sonnerat's *Travels,* Bk. 4, chapt. 2, 2B.[7])

Indeed, to the extent that we have insight into such matters, to the extent that we ourselves can investigate them, the dualist system has (though only given *a single* supremely good original being) from a *practical* point of view a preponderance of the argument in its favor as far as each man has to judge himself (though not as far as he is authorized to judge others); for to the extent of his knowledge of himself, reason provides him with no other view with respect to eternity than the one revealed at the end of life by his own conscience's sense of the moral [quality of the] life he has followed. But to make of that a *dogma,* thus a theoretical proposition that is valid in itself (objectively)—for that mere judgments of reason are far from sufficient. For what man knows himself so completely—who knows others so thoroughly—as to decide—after separating out from the causes of the purported good conduct of his life's course everything that one calls the wages of fortune, such as his innate good temperament, the naturally greater strength of his higher powers (of his understanding and reason to stay his impulses), and above all the occasions when chance fortunately spared him the temptations that others faced—after he separates all of this from his actual character (as he must necessarily do, in order to evaluate what belongs to it, for as a gift of fortune he cannot count these among his own merits), who then will be able to decide whether on the basis of his inner moral worth some man still has, in the all seeing eyes of a judge of the world, any advantage whatsoever over the others. And so, might it perhaps be nothing but an absurd self-conceit to speak of making this superficial self-knowledge the basis of any judgment in one's own favor, or in favor of someone else, regarding moral worth (and the fate it deserves)?[9] Consequently, the monistic as well as the dualistic systems, both regarded as dogma, appear to go utterly beyond the speculative capacity of human reason, and everything leads us back to strictly limiting those ideas of reason solely to the conditions of their practical use. For we as yet see nothing before us that could now teach us anything about our fate in a future world except the judgment of our own conscience, i.e., what, as far as we know it, our present moral state allows us rationally to judge that future to be. Thus, we assume that the principles (whether they have been good or bad) that we have found to govern the course of our moral life up until that end will also continue to do so after death, and we do not have the slightest reason to believe that they will be modified in that future time. Thus, we must expect an eternity in which there will be consequences governed by a good or bad principle commensurate with this merit or that guilt; from this perspective, it is wise to act *as if* another life and the moral state with which this one ends, along with its consequences, are unchangeable after one enters it. From a practical point of view, then, the assumed system must be the dualistic one; for, without wanting to determine which of the two systems merits theoretical and merely speculative preference, it appears that one is too easily lulled into casual security by the monistic system.

330

Why do men expect *an end* of the world *after all?* And why, if this is granted to them, do they expect an end that is terrible (for the greatest part of the human race)? . . . The basis for the *first* expectation appears to lie in this, that reason tells them that the duration of the world has a worth only insofar as the ultimate ends of the existence of rational beings can be met within it; but if these should not be attainable, creation itself would appear to those who believe in an end of the world to be as purposeless as a play that has no upshot whatsoever and has no rational design.[10] The *second* expectation is based on the belief in the human race's* fallen nature, a condition so extreme as to be beyond hope, for which the establishment of an end, an end that is indeed terrible, is the only appropriate provision of supreme wisdom and justice.[11] Therefore, all of the *omens of the youngest day* are also of the most terrifying kind (for when is an imagination, aroused by great expectations, lacking in signs and miracles?). Some see signs in increasing injustice, oppression of the poor by the wanton revelry of the rich, and the universal loss of honesty and faith, or in the bloody wars with which the entire Earth is inflamed, and so on; in a word, people see signs in a moral collapse and in a rapid rise of all the vices, along with their accompanying evils, of a sort that they fancy previous times have never seen. By contrast, others see signs in unaccustomed natural changes, in earthquakes, in storms, in floods, or in comets and atmospheric signs.

In fact, it is not without cause that men feel the burden of their existence, though they are themselves the cause of those burdens. The reason for this seems to me to lie in this.[12] In the natural progress of the human race, talents, skills, and tastes (along with its result, voluptuousness) become cultured before morality develops, and this state is precisely the most burdensome and dangerous one possible for morality, as well as for physical well-being, for needs grow much more vigorously than do the means to satisfy them. However, humanity's moral capacity (like Horace's *poena, pede claudo*),[13] which always lags behind, will someday overtake them (as one may hope to occur under a wise world ruler), though in its hasty course it becomes tangled in itself and often stumbles. Since our age enjoys an advantage that is based on experiential evidence as regards morality—at least

*In all times seeming sages (or philosophers), without paying properly appreciative attention to human nature's capacity for good, have worn themselves out in contemptuously portraying our earthly world, man's abode, in adverse and, in part, nauseating images. (1) As an *inn* (caravansary)—as that dervish sees it—where everyone who puts up there in the course of his life's journey must soon be pushed aside by one who follows. (2) As a *penitentiary*—an opinion to which the Brahmans, Tibetans and other oriental sages (as well as Plato) were attached—a place of punishment and purification for fallen spirits who were cast out of heaven and are now human or animal souls. (3) As an *insane asylum,* where not only does each person destroy his own intentions, but also each causes the others every imaginable heartfelt sorrow and, even more than that, takes the opportunity so to exercise his skill and power for the greatest of honors. Finally, (4) as a *cesspool* into which all the filth from other worlds has been

when our age is compared with all previous ones—man should be able
to feed on the hope that the youngest day may rather come in with Eli-
jah's ascension, bringing with it the end of all things, on Earth, than
with a descent to hell like that of Korah's horde.[14] However, this
heroic belief in virtue nonetheless appears subjectively not to have so
universally powerful an influence in the conversion of minds as does a
scene full of terror that is thought of as preceeding the last things.

*   *

*

Remark: Since it is with mere ideas that we are here dealing (or playing) with, ideas that reason itself creates and of which the objects (if
they have any) lie entirely beyond the scope of our vision, and
although these ideas transcend [*überschwenglich*] speculative cogni-
tion, they are not for that reason to be regarded as empty in every
regard. On the contrary, from the practical point of view, legislative
reason itself supplies us with them, and we are not to brood over what
their objects may be in and of themselves and in regard to their nature;
instead, we have to think of them with a view to moral principles con-   333
cerned with the ultimate purpose of all things (whereby these ideas,
which would otherwise be completely empty, acquire objective practical reality). Thus, we have before us an open field in which to
analyze and arrange this product of our own reason, the universal
concept of the end of all things, [and this must be done with an eye] to
the relation it bears to our cognitive faculty, as well as to classifying
those ideas that are subordinate to it.

Given this, the whole will be analyzed and presented in three sections: (1) in the *natural** end of all things, based on the divine
wisdom's ordering of moral ends, which we can *surely* understand
(from a practical point of view); (2) in the *mystical* (supernatural) end

---

dumped. This last inspiration is in a certain sense original, and we owe it to a Persian
wit, who placed paradise, the abode of the first human couple, in heaven; in this garden
there were to be found trees enough with an abundance of magnificent fruit, and after
they had been enjoyed, what remained of them disappeared in an unnoticeable evapora-
tion. In the midst of the garden was an exception, a single tree that bore alluring fruit
that could not be eliminated. Since our first parents longed to be allowed to taste it,
despite the command not to do so, and since they could not befoul heaven, there was no
other course than to follow the advice of an angel, who, pointing in the distance toward
the Earth, advised them in the following words, "That is the latrine for the whole
universe," and then lead them down into it so as to do what was necessary, and he then
flew back to heaven, leaving them behind. It is from that pair that the human race on
Earth sprang.

Natural (formaliter) means what necessarily follows according to laws in the particular order of which it is a member, consequently even in the moral order (thus, not
always only in the physical order). The *nonnatural*, which can be either the supernatural
or the contrary-to-natural, is contrasted with it. That which is necessary because of
natural causes would also be portrayed as materially natural (physically necessary).

of all things in the order of real causes, about which we *understand nothing;* (3) in the *contrary-to-nature* (perverse) end of all things, which we ourselves bring about inasmuch as we misunderstand the ultimate purpose of things. Of these, the first has been dealt with and the two still remaining follow.

*   *

*

In the *Apocalypse* (10:5–6)[15] [John writes,] "Then the angel . . . raised his right hand to heaven and swore by him who lives forever and ever, who created heaven and earth, etc., *that henceforth time shall no longer be."*

If one does not assume that this angel, "with his voice of seven thunders," (Rev. 10:3) did not want to shout nonsense, then he must have meant that henceforth there should be no *change,* for were there still change in the world, there would also be time, since change can occur only in time, and without the presupposition of time, nothing can be thought of.

Now this portrays an end to all things as objects of the senses that we are incapable of forming any concept of, since we become unavoidably enmeshed in contradiction whenever we desire to take one single step beyond the world of the senses into the intelligible world. And that is what happens here, for the moment that constitutes the end of the first is the very one in which the other should begin to be, and, consequently, the latter is placed in the same time sequence as the former, which is self-contradictory.

However, we also say that we can think an *unending* duration (for example, eternity), not because we may perhaps have some determinable concept of its extent—for that is impossible, since time is a wholly inadequate measure of it; instead—since where there is no time, there can also be *no end*—that concept is merely negative, a concept of eternal duration, whereby our knowledge is not advanced the length of a single step; indeed, in this we have only admitted that in regard to its (practical) objective, reason can never have done enough to attain its ultimate purpose by following the path of perpetual changes. Furthermore, reason would in its theoretical use be equally ineffective if it were to attempt to progress on the basis of a principle of the inactivity and unchangeability of the world's beings, but would, rather than progress, lapse into thoughtlessness. Nothing remains, then, for reason except to think of steady progress toward its ultimate purpose through a (temporally) unending process of change, in which instance its *character*[16] (which is not, like the world's beings, a phenomenon, but something supersensuous, consequently not changeable in time) remains permanently the same. The rule by which reason will abide in its practical use of this idea will say nothing other than that we must understand our maxims in such a way that through all the endlessly proceeding changes from good to better in our moral state, our character (the *homo noumenon,* whose behavior occurs in heaven) would not be subject to any temporal change whatsoever.

That, however, there will be some point in time when all change (and with it time itself) ceases, is a representation that offends the imagination. For then, surely, nature in its entirety will be fixed and, as it were, petrified; the last thought, the last feeling will come to a standstill in the thinking subject and remain, without change, always the same. For a being who is able to be conscious of its existence and its extent (as duration) only in time, such a life, if it can be called another life, must appear the same as [this] life's annihilation, for in order to think its way into such a state, a being such as ourselves must in general think of something, but *thinking* includes a [process of] reflection, which can itself only happen in time. Those who reside in that other world will, on the basis of the place where they reside (heaven or hell), be portrayed so as to be giving rise to the same eternal song—their Hallelujah!—or to the same eternal lament (Rev. 19:1-6, 20:15), which is intended to indicate the complete absence of all change in their state.   335

For all of that, this idea, which rises so far above our power to grasp, remains closely related to reason in its practical considerations. If we assume the best about mankind's morally physical state in this life, in particular, if we assume there to be a constant progress toward and approach to the supreme good (that is set out as his goal), mankind still (even with full consciousness of the unchangeableness of his character) cannot connect *contentedness* with the prospect of his state (both moral and physical) lasting through eternal change. For the state in which he is now always remains an evil one by comparison with the better one into which he is preparing himself to enter, and the representation of an unending progress toward the ultimate end is nonetheless at the same time one prospect in an unending sequence of evils, which, though they will surely be outweighed by the greater good, do not yet allow contentedness to prevail, a contentedness he can think of only by finally attaining the ultimate end.

Now the man who ponders these issues will lapse into *mysticism* (for reason, since it is not easily satisfied with its immanent, i.e., practical, use, though it gladly attempts something in the transcendent realm, also has its mysteries), where his reason does not understand itself and what it desires, but unfortunately strays—rather than limit itself, as is appropriate for a resident of a world of sense—to the boundaries of this world. From this tendency comes *Lao-kiun's*[17] monstrous system of the *supreme good,* which is supposed to consist of *nothingness* [*im Nichts*], i.e., in the consciousness derived from annihilating his personality, of *feeling* oneself flowing into and being swallowed up in the abyss of the divinity; and in order to have prior sensations of this state, Chinese philosophers exhaust themselves in dark rooms with their eyes closed trying to think and have sensations of their nothingness. From this tendency comes the *pantheism* (of the Tibetans and other Eastern peoples), and its metaphysical sublimation produced, with the same result, Spinozism: both have a close familial relation to the very ancient system according to which all human souls *emanate* from the divinity (and are ultimately reabsorbed into it). All of this [was put forth] for the sole reason that men might yet have some place

336   in which finally to enjoy *eternal rest,* which constitutes their purported blessed end of all things; but it is really a concept with which [the light of] reason goes out and all thinking itself ends.

*   *

*

The end of all things that pass through men's hands, even if they are used for good purposes, is foolishness, i.e., it is the use of means for the sake of purposes to which they are directly opposed. *Wisdom,* i.e., practical reason's application of wholly appropriate measures to the ultimate purpose of all things, resides only in God, though perhaps human wisdom could be regarded as not obviously acting contrary to this ultimate purpose.[18] However, to achieve this security against foolishness—something man may hope to do only by experiment and through frequent changes in his plans—is more "a treasure that even the best man can only chase, *if he wants perchance to lay hold of it;*"[19] and in this regard, he must never allow himself to be seized by selfish considerations, much less behave as if he *had laid hold* of it. From this come the attempts, which change from time to time and are often nonsensical, to find the proper means for making *an entire people's religion at one and the same time pure and powerful,* which makes one want to call out: "Poor mortals, among you nothing is constant, except inconstancy!"

If, in the meantime, even one of these attempts is finally so successful that the commonwealth is able and willing to listen not only to pious doctrine but also to the doctrine of enlightened practical reason (since it too is absolutely necessary to religion); if those among the people who are wise (in the human way) draw up plans that all persons can for the most part consent to—not making secret agreements among themselves (as clerics do) so as to demonstrate in a way that is beyond suspicion that they are concerned with truth; and if by virtue of a universal feeling of need to cultivate its moral capacity—a feeling not based on authority—the people, too, take an interest in these plans as a whole (if not in the smallest detail); then nothing would appear to be more advisable than to permit those wise men to set out and pursue their course, since they are, for once, making good progress in regard to this idea that they are pursuing. But it must be left up to

337   providence to choose the means in regard to the best ultimate end, since, as this must result from the course of nature, what those means are always remains uncertain. For no matter how difficult to believe it

may be, where it is absolutely impossible to see with certainty in advance the result of particular means that are accepted on the basis of all human wisdom (which, if it is to be true to its name, must proceed solely toward morality), one must in a practical way believe in a concurrence between divine wisdom and the course of nature, if one is not to give up one's cherished ultimate purpose.[20] Someone will surely object: It has often been said that the present plan is the best; one must abide by it now and forever; what exists now does so for eternity. "Whoever (on the basis of this concept) is good, is eternally good, and whoever (contrary to him) is bad, is eternally bad." (Rev. 22:11) It is just as if eternity and, along with it, the end of all things could already enter at this time; nonetheless, since the time [of that scriptural statement] there have been constant new [final] plans to put us back on the road—and among them the newest was often only the revival of an old one; and in the future there will also be no lack of more *final* attempts.

I am so very conscious of my inability to make a new, successful attempt in this regard, that I, being in possession of no great imagination, might rather advise persons to leave these matters just as they last stood, since for almost a generation they have proved reasonably good in their results. But because that may not be the view of men whose spirit is either great or venturesome, permit me to comment discreetly not so much on what they would have to do, but, instead, on what they must pay attention to so as not to offend, since they would otherwise act contrary to their own intention (even if it were the best).

In addition to the highest respect that the holiness of its laws irresistibly inspires, there is in Christianity something *worthy of love*. (Here I do not mean the worthiness of love of a person, which it procured for us at great sacrifice, but rather that of the matter itself, namely, the moral constitution that He founded, for the former is only a result of the latter.) Respect is without doubt primary, for without it genuine love cannot arise, though one can cultivate great respect for another, even without loving that person. However, if it is a question not just of the representation of duty [*Pflichtvorstellung*], but also of observing duty [*Pflichtbefolgung*]—if we ask about the *subjective* basis of actions, from which, if one may assume it to exist, one is first [able] 338 to expect what a man *will do,* and not merely after the objective basis of actions, which [inform us regarding] *what he ought to do*—then is love, as the free integration of the will of another into one's maxims, an indispensable addition to human nature's imperfection (to that aspect of it whereby man must be coerced to do what by virtue of laws reason prescribes to human nature). For what one does not do gladly he does so grudgingly—even to the point of sophistical pretext to avoid duty's command—that this incentive [of duty] cannot be counted on to any great degree unless the command is accompanied by love.

If, in order to perfect it, one now adds to Christianity some further authority (even if it, too, is divine), no matter how well-meaning the intention, or how good the purpose, Christianity's worthiness of love has still faded away, for it is contradictory to *command* someone not only to do something but to do it willingly.

Christianity's objective is to promote love of the concern for observing one's duty, and in addition it elicits this love, for its founder speaks not as a commander who requires obedience to *his will,* but as a friend of mankind who places in the hearts of his fellow men their own well-understood wills, i.e., the will in accord with which they would themselves freely act.

Thus, it is the liberal state of mind [*Denkungart*]—as distant from the slave's as from the anarchist's mentality—that Christianity expects its doctrine to affect, for by its doctrine it hopes to win the hearts of men, as it has already enlightened their understandings with its representation of the law of their duty. The feeling of freedom in choosing ultimate ends is what for them makes legislation worthy of love. Thus, although the teacher of that doctrine also ushers in *punishments,* still that is not to be understood in such a way as to make these the incentives for following its commands; at least it is not in keeping with the true nature of Christianity to explain them in this way, for if it were, Christianity would cease being worthy of love. One may instead regard it only as a loving warning, one that springs from the goodness of the will of the legislator, to guard against the damage that must inevitably spring from transgressing the law (for: *lex est surda et inexorabilis.* Livy),[21] because it is not Christianity as a freely accepted body of maxims for living one's life that threatens us here, but the law, which, as an unchangeable order that lies in the nature of things, does not leave it up even to the Creator's will to decide whether its consequences will be thus or otherwise.

If Christianity promises *rewards* (e.g. "Accept it with gladness and exultation, for you have a rich reward in Heaven")[22] that must not, according to the liberal way of thinking, be set out as if it were an offer *to bribe* men to pursue a good course of life; for if it were, Christianity would not be intrinsically worthy of love. Only a demand for such actions as spring from unselfish motives [*Beweggründen*] can inspire in men respect for him who makes the demand; but without respect there is no true love. Thus, one must not attribute a meaning to those promises that would require regarding those rewards as incentives [*Triebfedern*] for action. The love that binds the liberal way of thinking to a benefactor is not guided by the goods that the needy receive, but only by the goodness of the *will* of him who enjoys offering them, even if he should perhaps not be able to do so, or even if he is prevented from doing so by other motives that arise from considering what is best for the world as a whole.

That is the moral worthiness of love that Christianity carries within itself, a worthiness that still glimmers through the many external constraints added to it by frequent changes of opinion. This worthiness has sustained Christianity in the face of the dislike that it must other-

339

wise have met, and (what is remarkable) in this time of man's greatest enlightenment Christianity shines forth with a light only so much the greater for this worthiness.

Should Christianity ever reach the point where it ceases to be worthy of love (which could well come about if instead of its gentle spirit it were armed with dictatorial authority), then dislike and resistance must govern man's attitude toward it, for there is no neutrality (and still less coalition among contradictory principles) when it comes to moral matters; and the *antichrist,* who is taken as the harbinger of the youngest day, would begin his certainly short regime (presumably based on fear and selfishness), because in that instance, while Christianity was indeed *determined* to be the world's universal religion, it would not be *favored* by fate to become so. And from a moral point of view the (perverse) *end of all things* would make its entrance.

Notes for
The End of All Things

References to essays in this volume are to page numbers in the *margins*.

1. A. A. VIII, 325–339. *The End of All Things* first appeared in the *Berlinische Monatsscrift,* June, 1794.

2. Albrecht von Haller (1708–1777) *Unvollkommenes Gedicht über die Ewigkeit (Imperfect Poems on Eternity),* 1736.

3. "Those who stood by could not satisfy their deep desire to look at those terrible eyes." Vergil, *Aeneid,* VIII, 265, trans. L.R. Lind.

4. This idiom *"jüngster Tag"* ("youngest day") is peculiar to German and has no real cognate in English. Since Kant's text explains its meaning I have chosen to let it stand instead of attempting to find some idiomatic English expression to use in its place. The paradoxes that Kant develops in the next several paragraphs regarding the very concept of an end of time are characteristic of the puzzles concerning space and time that provided impetus to formulate his theory that they must be among the forms that knowing subjects like ourselves must impose on sensuous awareness so as to structure and organize it. See *Prolegomena,* 280–294, and A 22/B 37 – A 49/B 66–73.

5. See Rev. 6:14.

6. Kant carefully distinguishes between the sphere of the sensuous, about which it is possible for beings such as ourselves to have what he calls cognitive knowledge (*Erkenntnis*), and the sphere of the supersensuous, about which we can think, but not have cognitive knowledge. See A 50/B 74 – A 52/B 76 and A 312/B 368 – A 332/B 389.

7. Sonnerat, (1749–1814) *Reise nach Ostindien und China auf Befehl des Königs unternommen v Jahr 1774 bis 1781, (Travels to East India and China During 1774–1781 Undertaken at the King's Command)* Zurich, 1783, 2 vols. Compare this note with the one on pp. 359–60.

8. See Gen. 18.

9. See *Theory and Practice,* 284.

10. See *Theory and Practice,* 308 f.

11. See *Spec. Beg. Human History,* 123.

12. See *Spec. Beg. Human History,* 116–117 n.

13. "Raro antecedentem scelestum/Deseruit pede Poena claudo." ("but rarely does vengeance, albeit of halting gait, fail to o'ertake the guilty, though he gain the start.") Horace, *Odes* III, 2.32, trans. E.E. Bennett, Loeb Classical Library.

14. See 2 Kings 2:11 and Num. 16:32 respectively.

15. I.e., Revelation.

16. See *Critique of Pure Reason,* A 538/B 566 - A 541/B 569. The term Kant uses here is *Gesinnung,* which does not mean "character" in ordinary German usage; however, evidence internal to the *Critique of Pure Reason* and other critical writings strongly suggest that he uses this term and *Charakter* as rough synonyms. See A 746/B 774 - A 748/B 776.

17. The Chinese philosopher of "the way," Lao-Tzu (604–531 B.C.).

18. See *Theory and Practice,* 288–89.

19. Phil. 3:12-14.

20. See *Spec. Beg. Human History,* 120 f., *Theory and Practice,* 310, and *Perpetual Peace,* 365.

21. "Law is a given and is inexorable." The passage in the original reads: "leges rem surdam, inexorabilem esse, salubriorem, melioremque inopi quam potenti." ("The law was a thing without ears, inexorable, more salutary and serviceable to the pauper than to the great man.") Livy II. 3.4, trans. B.O. Foster, Loeb Classical Library.

22. Matt. 5:12.

Zum

ewigen Frieden.

Ein philosophischer Entwurf

von

Immanuel Kant.

Königsberg,
bey Friedrich Nicolovius.
1795.

Whether this satirical inscription on a certain Dutch shopkeeper's sign, on which a graveyard was painted, holds for *men* in general, or especially for heads of state who can never get enough of war, or perhaps only for philosophers who dream that sweet dream, is not for us to decide. However, the author of this essay does set out one condition: The practical politician tends to look down with great smugness on the political theorist, regarding him as an academic whose empty ideas cannot endanger the nation [*Staat*],[2] since the nation must proceed on principles [derived from] experience [*Erfahrungsgrundsätzen*]; consequently, the theorist is allowed to fire his entire volley, without the *worldly-wise* statesman becoming the least bit concerned. Now if he is to be consistent—and this is the condition I set out—the practical politician must not claim, in the event of a dispute with a theorist, to detect some danger to the nation in those views that the political theorist expresses openly and without ulterior motive. By this *clausula salvatoria,* the author of this essay will regard himself to be expressly protected in the best way possible from all malicious interpretation.

First Section
Which Contains the Preliminary Articles for Perpetual Peace Among Nations

1. No treaty of peace that tacitly reserves issues for a future war shall be held valid.[3]

For if this were the case, it would be a mere truce, a suspension of hostilities, not *peace,* which means the end of all hostilities, so much so that even to modify it by "perpetual" smacks of pleonasm. A peace treaty nullifies all existing causes for war, even if they are unknown to the contracting parties, and even if they are assiduously ferreted out from archival documents. When one or both parties to a peace treaty, being too exhausted to continue the war, has a mental reservation (*reservatio mentalis*) concerning some presently unmentioned pretension that will be revived at the first opportune moment, since ill will between the warring parties still remains, that reservation is a bit of mere Jesuitical casuistry. If we judge such actions in their true character, they are beneath the dignity of a ruler, just as a willingness to indulge in reasoning of this sort is beneath his minister's dignity.

344

If, however, enlightened concepts of political prudence lead us to believe that the true honor of a nation lies in its continual increase of power by whatever means necessary, this judgment will appear academic and pedantic.

2.   No independent nation, be it large or small, may be acquired by another nation by inheritance, exchange, purchase, or gift.

A nation is not (like the ground on which it is located) a possession (*partrimonium*). It is a society of men whom no one other than the nation itself can command or dispose of. Since, like a tree, each nation has its own roots, to incorporate it into another nation as a graft, denies its existence as a moral person, turns it into a thing, and thus contradicts the concept of the original contract, without which a people [*Volk*] has no rights.* Everyone is aware of the danger that this purported right of acquisition by the marriage of nations to one another—a custom unknown in other parts of the world—has brought to Europe, even in the most recent times. It is a new form of industry, in which influence is increased without expending energy, and territorial possessions are extended merely by establishing family alliances. The hiring out of the troops of one nation to another for use against an enemy not common to both of them falls under this principle, for by this practice subjects are used and wasted as mere objects to be manipulated at will.

345   3.   Standing armies (*miles perpetuus*) shall be gradually abolished.

For they constantly threaten other nations with war by giving the appearance that they are prepared for it, which goads nations into competing with one another in the number of men under arms, and this practice knows no bounds. And since the costs related to maintaining peace will in this way finally become greater than those of a short war, standing armies are the cause of wars of aggression that are intended to end burdensome expenditures.[5] Moreover, paying men to kill or be killed appears to use them as mere machines and tools in the hands of another (the nation), which is inconsistent with the rights of humanity [*Menschheit*]. The voluntary, periodic military training of citizens so that they can secure their homeland against external aggression is an entirely different matter. The same could be said about the hoarding of treasure (for of the three sorts of power, the *power of an army,* the *power of alliance,* and the *power of money,* the third is the most reliable instrument of war). Thus, except for the difficulty in discovering the amount of wealth another nation possesses, the hoarding

*A hereditary monarchy is not a nation that can be inherited by another nation; only the right to rule it can be inherited by another physical person. Consequently, the nation acquires a ruler, but the ruler as such (i.e., as one who already has another kingdom) does not acquire the nation.[4]

of treasure could be regarded as preparation for war that necessitates aggression.

4. No national debt shall be contracted in connection with the foreign affairs of the nation.

Seeking either internal or external help for the national economy (e.g., for improvement of roads, new settlements, storage of food against years of bad harvest, and so on) is above suspicion. However, as an instrument in the struggle among powers, the credit system—the ingenious invention of a commercial people [England] during this century—of endlessly growing debts that remain safe against immediate demand (since the demand for payment is not made by all creditors at the same time) is a dangerous financial power. It is a war chest exceeding the treasure of all other nations taken together, and it can be exhausted only by an inevitable default in taxes (although it can also be forestalled indefinitely by the economic stimulus that derives from credit's influence on industry and commerce). This ease in making war, combined with the inclination of those in power to do so—an inclination that seems innate in human nature—is a great obstacle to perpetual peace. Thus, forbidding foreign debt must be a preliminary 346 article for perpetual peace, for eventual yet unavoidable national bankruptcy must entangle many innocent nations, and that would clearly injure them. Consequently, other nations are justified in allying themselves against such a nation and its pretensions.

5. No nation shall forcibly interfere with the constitution and government of another.

For what can justify its doing so? Perhaps some offense that one nation's subjects give to those of another? Instead, this should serve as a warning by providing an example of the great evil that a people falls into through its lawlessness. Generally, the bad example that one free person furnishes for another (as a *scandalum acceptum*) does not injure the latter. But it would be different if, as a result of internal discord, a nation were divided in two and each part, regarding itself as a separate nation, lay claim to the whole; for (since they are in a condition of anarchy) the aid of a foreign nation to one of the parties could not be regarded as interference by the other in its constitution. So long, however, as this internal conflict remains undecided, a foreign power's interference would violate the rights of an independent people struggling with its internal ills. Doing this would be an obvious offense and would render the autonomy of every nation insecure.

6. No nation at war with another shall permit such acts of war as shall make mutual trust impossible during some future time of peace: Such acts include the use of *Assassins* (*percussores*)

Poisoners (venefici) breach of surrender, instigation of treason (perduellio) in the opposing nation, etc.

These are dishonorable stratagems. Some level of trust in the enemy's way of thinking [*Denkungsart*] must be preserved even in the midst of war, for otherwise no peace can ever be concluded and the hostilities would become a war of extermination (*bellum internecinum*). Yet war is but a sad necessity in the state of nature (where no tribunal empowered to make judgments supported by the power of law exists), one that maintains the rights of a nation by mere might, where neither party can be declared an unjust enemy (since this already presupposes a judgment of right) and the outcome of the conflict (as if it were a so-called "judgment of God") determines the side on which justice lies. A war of punishment (*bellum punitivum*) between nations is inconceivable (for there is no relation of superior and inferior between them). From this it follows that a war of extermination—where the destruction of both parties along with all rights is the result—would permit perpetual peace to occur only in the vast graveyard of humanity as a whole. Thus, such a war, including all means used to wage it, must be absolutely prohibited. But that the means named above inexorably lead to such war becomes clear from the following: Once they come into use, these intrinsically despicable, infernal acts cannot long be confined to war alone. This applies to the use of spies (*uti exploratoribus*), where only the dishonorableness *of others* (which can never be entirely eliminated) is exploited; but such activities will also carry over to peacetime and will thus undermine it.

347

*   *

*

Although the laws set out above are objectively, i.e., from the perspective of the intention of those in power, merely *prohibitive laws* (*leges prohibitivae*), some of them are of that *strict* kind—that is, of that class of laws that holds regardless of the circumstances (*leges strictae*)—that demands *immediate* implementation (*viz.,* Nos. 1, 5, and 6). However, others (*viz.,* Nos. 2, 3, 4), while not exceptions to the rule of law, do permit, depending on circumstances, some subjective leeway in their *implementation* (*leges latae*) as long as one does not lose sight of their end. This permission, e.g., of the *restoration* of freedom to certain nations in accord with No. 2, cannot be put off until doomsday (or as Augustus was wont to promise, *ad calendas graecas*), that is, we cannot fail to implement them. Delay is permitted only to prevent such premature implementation as might injure the intention of the article. For in the case of the second article, the prohibition concerns only the *mode of acquisition,* which is henceforth forbidden, but not the *state of ownership,* which, though not supported by the necessary title of right, was at the time (of the putative acquisition) accepted as lawful by public opinion in all nations.*

Second Section

Which Contains the Definitive Articles

for Perpetual Peace Among Nations

348

The state of peace among men living in close proximity is not the natural state (*status naturalis*); instead, the natural state is a one of war, which does not just consist in open hostilities, but also in the constant and enduring threat of them.[7] The state of peace must therefore be *established,* for the suspension of hostilities does not provide the security of peace, and unless this security is pledged by one neighbor to another (which can happen only in a state of *lawfulness*), the latter, from whom such security has been requested, can treat the former as an enemy.†

349

*It has previously been doubted, not unjustifiably, whether in addition to *commands* (*leges praeceptivae*) and *prohibitions* (*leges prohibitivae*) pure reason could provide *permissive laws* (*leges permissivae*). For in general laws contain a foundation of objective practical necessity, while permission only provides a foundation for certain acts that depend on practical contingencies [*Zufälligkeit*]. Thus a *permissive law* would necessitate an action that one cannot be compelled to perform, which, if the object of law has the same sense in both cases, would entail a contradiction. But the permissive law here under consideration only prohibits certain modes of acquiring a right in the future (e.g., through inheritance), while the exception from this prohibition, i.e., the permission, applies to a present state of possession. In the transition from the state of nature to that of civil society, then, this possession, while unjust in itself, may nonetheless be regarded as *honest* (*possessio putativa*) and can continue to endure by virtue of a permissive law derived from natural right. However, as soon as any putative possession comes to be regarded as prohibited in the state of nature, every similar form of acquisition is subsequently prohibited in civil society, and this putative right to continuing possession would not hold if such a supposed acquisition had occurred in the civil state. In that case it would, as an offense against natural law, have to cease existing as soon as its illegality were discovered.

348

My desire here has been simply to draw the attention of proponents of natural right to the concept of a *lex permissiva*, a concept that reason in its systematically analytic use sets out and that is often used in civil (statutory) law, though with this difference, namely, that the prohibitive part of law stands on its own, while the permissive part is not (as it should be) included in the law as a limiting condition, but is regarded instead as among the exceptions to it. This means that this or that will be forbidden, *as is the case with Nos. 1, 2, and 3, and so on indefinitely, for permissions arise only circumstantially, not according to a principle, that is, they arise only in considering specific situations. Otherwise the conditions would have to be stated in the *formulation of the prohibitive laws* and would in that way have to become laws of permission. It is therefore regrettable that the incisive, but unsolved Prize question posed by the wise and acute Count von Windischgrätz,[6] a question that directly concerns this issue, has been forgotten so quickly. For the possibility of a formula (such as exists in mathematics) is the only true criterion of all subsequent legislation, and without it the so-called *ius certum* will forever remain a pious wish. In its absence, we shall merely have *general* laws (which are valid in general), but no universal ones (which are universally valid), and it is the latter that the concept of a law requires.

†It is commonly assumed that one ought not take hostile action against another unless one has already been actively *injured* by that person and that is entirely correct if

First Definitive Article of Perpetual Peace
The civil constitution of every nation should be republican.

The sole established constitution that follows from the idea [*Idee*] of an original contract, the one on which all of a nation's just [*rechtliche*][8] legislation must be based, is republican. For, first, it accords with the principles of the *freedom* of the members of a society (as men), second, it accords with the principles of the *dependence* of everyone on a single, common [source of] legislation (as subjects), and third, it accords with the law of the equality of them all (as citizens).*
Thus, so far as [the matter of] right is concerned, republicanism is the

350

---

both parties live in a state [governed by] *civil law.* For by entering into civil society, each person gives every other (by virtue of the sovereignty that has power over them both) the requisite security. However, a man (or a people) who is merely in a state of nature denies me this security and injures me merely by being in this state. For although he does not actively (*facto*) injure me, he does so by virtue of the lawlessness of his state (*statu iniusto*), by which he constantly threatens me, and I can require him either to enter with me into a state of civil law or to remove himself from my surroundings. Thus, the postulate on which all the following articles rest is: "All men who can mutually influence one another must accept some civil constitution."

Every just constitution, as far as the persons who accept it are concerned, will be one of the three following:

1. one conforming to the civil rights of men in a nation (*ius civitatis*);
2. one conforming to the *rights of nations* in relation to one another;
3. one conforming to the *rights of world citizenship,* sofar as men and nations stand in mutually influential relations as citizens of a universal nation of men (*ius cosmopoliticum*). These are not arbitrary divisions, but ones that are necessary in relationship to the idea [*Idee*] of perpetual peace. Because if even only one of these [nations] had only physical influence on another, they would be in a state of nature, and consequently they would be bound together in a state of war. Our intention here is to free them from this.

*Rightful [*Rechtliche*] (consequently external) *freedom* cannot be defined in the way it usually is, as the privilege to do whatever one will as long as one does no injustice. For what does privilege [*Befugnis*] mean? The possibility of action as long as one does no wrong. Thus, the clarification would read: Freedom is the possibility of action as long as one does no wrong. One does no wrong (one may thus do what one wills), if only one does no wrong. This is a mere empty tautology. Instead, external (*rightful*) *freedom* is to be clarified as follows: it is the privilege not to obey any external laws except those to which I have been able to give my consent. In just the same way, external (*rightful*) *equality* in a nation is that relation among citizens whereby no citizen can be bound by a law, unless all are subject to it simultaneously and in the very same way. (The principle of *rightful* dependence requires no clarification, for it is already contained in the concept of a political constitution in general.) The validity of these innate rights that necessarily and inalienably belong to humanity [*Menschheit*] is confirmed and raised to an even higher level by virtue of the principle that man has rightful relations to higher beings [*Wesen*] (if he believes in them), since by these very same principles he represents himself as a citizen in the supersensuous world. Now so far as my freedom is concerned, I have no obligation even to divine laws knowable only by reason, except only insofar as I am able to consent to them. (For it is through the law of freedom that I am first able rationally to create a concept of the divine will.) But as regards the principle of equality, even the highest worldly being that I can think of (say a great Aeon)—but excepting God—has no reason (assuming I perform my duty in my position, as that Aeon performs his duty in his) to expect it to be my duty only to obey, leaving the right of command to him. This principle of *equality* does not (as does that of freedom) pertain to one's relation to God because God is the sole being excepted from the concept of

original foundation of all forms of civil constitution. Thus, the only question remaining is this, does it also provide the only foundation for perpetual peace?

Now in addition to the purity of its origin, a purity whose source is the pure concept of right, the republican constitution also provides for this desirable result, namely, perpetual peace, and the reason for this is as follows: If (as must inevitably be the case, given this form of constitution) the consent of the citizenry is required in order to determine whether or not there will be war, it is natural that they consider all its calamities before committing themselves to so risky a game. (Among these are doing the fighting themselves, paying the costs of war from their own resources, having to repair at great sacrifice the war's devastation, and, finally, the ultimate evil that would make peace itself better, never being able—because of new and constant wars—to expunge the burden of debt.) By contrast, under a nonrepublican constitution, where subjects are not citizens, the easiest thing in the world to do is to declare war. Here the ruler is not a fellow citizen, but the nation's owner, and war does not affect his table, his hunt, his places of pleasure, his court festivals, and so on. Thus, he can decide to go to war for the most meaningless of reasons, as if it were a kind of pleasure party, and he can blithely leave its justification (which decency requires) to his diplomatic corps, who are always prepared for such exercises. 351

*   *

*

The following comments are necessary to prevent confusing (as so often happens) the republican form of constitution with the democratic one: The forms of a nation (*civitas*) can be analyzed either on the basis of the persons who possess the highest political authority or on the basis of the way the people are *governed* by their ruler, whoever he may be. The first is called the form of sovereignty [*Beherrschung*] (*forma imperii*), of which only three kinds are possible, specifically, where either *one,* or *several* in association, or *all* those together who make up civil society possess the sovereign power (Autocracy, Aristo- 352

duty.

Concerning all citizens' right of equality as subjects, one can resolve the issue of whether a hereditary nobility is permissible by asking whether some rank making one citizen superior to another granted by the nation is antecedent to *merit,* or whether merit must precede rank. Now clearly, when rank is tied to birth it is completely uncertain whether merit (skill and integrity in one's office) will accompany it. Consequently, this hereditary arrangement is no different from conferring command on some favorite person who is wholly lacking in merit. This is something that the general will of a people would never agree to in an original contract (which is the principle that underlies all rights). For a nobleman is not, by virtue of that fact alone, a *noble* man. Concerning the *nobility of office* (as one can designate the rank of a higher magistrate, which one must earn by virtue of merit), here rank does not belong to the person, but to the position he holds, and this does not violate [the principle of] equality, because when that person resigns his office he gives up his rank at the same time and again becomes one of the people. 351

3

cracy and Democracy, the power of a monarch, the power of a nobility, the power of a people). The second is the form of government (*forma regiminis*) and concerns the way in which a nation, based on its
constitution (the act of the general will whereby a group becomes a
people), exercises its authority. In this regard, government is either
republican or *despotic. Republicanism* is that political principle
whereby executive power (the government) is separated from legislative power. In a despotism the ruler independently executes laws that it
has itself made; here rulers have taken hold of the public will and
treated it as their own private will. Among the three forms of government, *democracy,* in the proper sense of the term, is necessarily a
despotism, because it sets up an executive power in which all citizens
make decisions about and, if need be, against one (who therefore does
not agree); consequently, all, who are not quite all, decide, so that the
general will contradicts both itself and freedom.

Every form of government that is not *representative* is properly
speaking *without form,* because one and the same person can no more
be at one and the same time the legislator and executor of his will
(than the universal proposition can serve as the major premise in a
syllogism and at the same time be the subsumption of the particular
under it in the minor premise). And although the other two forms of
political constitution are defective inasmuch as they always leave
room for a democratic form of government, it is nonetheless possible
that they assume a form of government that accords with the *spirit* of
a representative system: As Friederick II[9] at least *said,* "I am merely
353   the nation's highest servant."* The democratic system makes this impossible, for everyone wants to rule. One can therefore say, the
smaller the number of persons who exercise the power of the nation
(the number of rulers), the more they represent and the closer the
political constitution approximates the possibility of republicanism,
and thus, the constitution can hope through gradual reforms finally to
become republican. For this reason, attaining this state that embodies
a completely just constitution is more difficult in an aristocracy than
in a monarchy, and, except by violent revolution, there is no possibility of attaining it in a democracy. Nonetheless, the people are incomparably more concerned with the form of government† than with the

---

*People have often criticized the lofty titles that are normally bestowed on a ruler
("the divinely annointed" and "the representative and executor of the divine will on
earth") as gross and extravagant flatteries; but it seems to me that this is without basis.
353   Far from stirring arrogance in the ruler of a country, they should instead humble his
soul, providing he possesses reason (which one must assume) and has reflected on the
fact that he has undertaken an office that is too great for a single man, the holiest one
that God has established on earth, the protector of the *rights of mankind,* and he must
always be careful not to tread upon this apple of God's eye.

†In his important sounding but hollow and empty language, Mallet du Pan,[10] boasts
of having after many years of experience finally come to be convinced of Pope's well
known saying, "For forms of government let fools contest;/Whate're is best admini-

form of the constitution (although a great deal depends on the degree
to which the latter is suited to the goals of the former). But if the form
of government is to cohere with the concept of right, it must include
the representative system, which is possible only in a republican form
of government and without which (no matter what the constitution
may be) government is despotic and brutish. None of the ancient so-
called republics were aware of this, and consequently they inevitably
degenerated into despotism; still, this is more bearable under a single
person's rulership than other forms of government are.

Second Definitive Article for a Perpetual Peace   354
The right of nations shall be based on a federation of free states.

As nations, peoples can be regarded as single individuals who injure
one another through their close proximity while living in the state of
nature (i.e., independently of external laws). For the sake of its own
security, each nation can and should demand that the others enter into
a contract resembling the civil one and guaranteeing the rights of each.
This would be a federation *of nations,* but it must not be a nation consisting of nations. The latter would be contradictory, for in every nation there exists the relation of *ruler* (legislator) to *subject* (those who
obey, the people); however, many nations in a single nation would
constitute only a single nation, which contradicts our assumption
(since we are here weighing the rights of *nations* in relation to one
another, rather than fusing them into a single nation).

Just as we view with deep disdain the attachment of savages to their
lawless freedom—preferring to scuffle without end rather than to
place themselves under lawful restraints that they themselves constitute, consequently preferring a mad freedom to a rational one—and
consider it barbarous, rude, and brutishly degrading of humanity, so
also should we think that civilized peoples (each one united into a nation) would hasten as quickly as possible to escape so similar a state of
abandonment. Instead, however, each *nation* sees its majesty (for it is
absurd to speak of the majesty of a people) to consist in not being subject to any external legal constraint, and the glory of its ruler consists
in being able, without endangering himself, to command many thou-
sands to sacrifice themselves for a matter that does not concern

---

stered is best.''[11] If that means that the best administered government is the best administered, then he has, in Swift's expression, "cracked a nut and been rewarded with
only a worm." But if it means that it is the best form of government, i.e., political constitution, then it is fundamentally false, for good governments prove nothing about
form of government. Who has ruled better than a Titus and a Marcus Aurelius, and yet
one was succeeded by a Domitian and the other by Commodus, which could not have
happened under a good political constitution, since their unfitness for the post was
known early enough and the power of the ruler was sufficient to have excluded them
from it.

them.* The primary difference between European and American savages is this, that while many of the latter tribes have been completely
eaten by their enemies, the former know how to make better use of
those they have conquered than to consume them: they increase the
number of their subjects and thus also the quantity of instruments
they have to wage even more extensive wars.

Given the depravity of human nature, which is revealed and can be
glimpsed in the free relations among nations (though deeply concealed
by governmental restraints in law governed civil-society), one must
wonder why the word *right* has not been completely discarded from
the politics of war as pedantic, or why no nation has openly ventured
to declare that it should be. For while Hugo Grotius, Pufendorf, Vattel,[12] and others whose philosophically and diplomatically formulated
codes do not and cannot have the slightest legal force (since nations do
not stand under any common external constraints), are always piously
cited in justification of a war of aggression (and who therefore provide only cold comfort), no example can be given of a nation having
foregone its intention [of going to war] based on the arguments provided by such important men. The homage that every nation pays (at
least in words) to the concept of right proves, nonetheless, that there is
in man a still greater, though presently dormant, moral aptitude to
master the evil principle in himself (a principle he cannot deny) and to
hope that others will also overcome it. For otherwise the word *right*
would never leave the mouths of those nations that want to make war
on one another, unless it were used mockingly, as when that Gallic
prince declared, "Nature has given the strong the prerogative of making the weak obey them."

Nations can press for their rights only by waging war and never in a
trial before an independent tribunal, but war and its favorable consequence, victory, cannot determine the right. And although a *treaty of
peace* can put an end to some particular war, it cannot end the state of
war (the tendency always to find a new pretext for war). (And this
situation cannot straightforwardly be declared unjust, since in this cir-
cumstance each nation is judge of its own case.) Nor can one say of
nations as regards their rights what one can say concerning the natural
rights of men in a state of lawlessness, to wit, that "they should aban-
don this state." (For as nations they already have an internal, legal
constitution and therefore have outgrown the compulsion to subject
themselves to another legal constitution that is subject to someone
else's concept of right.) Nonetheless, from the throne of its moral
legislative power, reason absolutely condemns war as a means of
determining the right and makes seeking the state of peace a matter of
unmitigated duty. But without a contract among nations peace can be

---

*Thus a Bulgarian prince gave this answer to a Greek emperor who kindly offered to
settle a conflict between them by a duel: "A smith who has tongs will not use his hands
to take the glowing iron from the fire."

neither inaugurated nor guaranteed. A league of a special sort must therefore be established, one that we can call a *league of peace* (*foedus pacificum*), which will be distinguished from a *treaty of peace* (*pactum pacis*) because the latter seeks merely to stop *one* war, while the former seeks to end *all* wars forever. This league does not seek any power of the sort possessed by nations, but only the maintenance and security of each nation's own freedom, as well as that of the other nations leagued with it, without their having thereby to subject themselves to civil laws and their constraints (as men in the state of nature must do). It can be shown that this *idea of federalism* should eventually include all nations and thus lead to perpetual peace. For if good fortune should so dispose matters that a powerful and enlightened people should form a republic (which by its nature must be inclined to seek perpetual peace), it will provide a focal point for a federal association among other nations that will join it in order to guarantee a state of peace among nations that is in accord with the idea of the right of nations, and through several associations of this sort such a federation can extend further and further.

That a people might say, "There should be no war among us, for we want to form ourselves into a nation, i.e., place ourselves under a supreme legislative, executive, and judicial power to resolve our conflicts peacefully," is understandable. But when a nation says, "There should be no war between me and other nations, though I recognize no supreme legislative power to guarantee me my rights and him his," then if there does not exist a surrogate of the union in a civil society, which is a free federation, it is impossible to understand what the basis for so entrusting my rights is. Such a federation is necessarily tied rationally to the concept of the right of nations, at least if this latter notion has any meaning.

The concept of the right of nations as a right to go to war is meaningless (for it would then be the right to determine the right not by independent, universally valid laws that restrict the freedom of everyone, but by one-sided maxims backed by force). Consequently, the concept of the right of nations must be understood as follows: that it serves justly those men who are disposed to seek one another's destruction and thus to find perpetual peace in the grave that covers all the horrors of violence and its perpetrators. Reason can provide related nations with no other means for emerging from the state of lawlessness, which consists solely of war, than that they give up their savage (lawless) freedom, just as individual persons do, and, by accommodating themselves to the constraints of common law, establish a *nation of peoples* (*civitas gentium*) that (continually growing) will finally include all the people of the earth. But they do not will to do this because it does not conform to their idea of the right of nations, and consequently they discard in *hypothesis* what is true in *thesis*. So (if everything is not to be lost) in place of the positive idea of *a world republic* they put only the *negative* surrogate of an enduring, ever ex-

357

panding *federation* that prevents war and curbs the tendency of that
hostile inclination to defy the law, though there will always be constant danger of their breaking loose. (*Furor impius intus—fremit hor-
ridus ore cruento.* Vergil)* [13]

(handwritten: won'ed/peace fragile/)

Third Definitive Article for a Perpetual Peace
Cosmopolitan right shall be limited to conditions
of universal *hospitality*.

358   As in the preceding articles, our concern here is not with philan-
thropy, but with *right,* and in this context *hospitality* (hospitableness)
means the right of an alien not to be treated as an enemy upon his ar-
rival in another's country. If it can be done without destroying him, he
can be turned away; but as long as he behaves peaceably he cannot be
treated as an enemy. He may request the *right* to be a *permanent
visitor* (which would require a special, charitable agreement to make
him a fellow inhabitant for a certain period), but the *right to visit,* to
associate, belongs to all men by virtue of their common ownership of
the earth's surface; for since the earth is a globe, they cannot scatter
themselves infinitely, but must, finally, tolerate living in close proximity, because originally no one had a greater right to any region of
the earth than anyone else. Uninhabitable parts of this surface—the
sea and deserts—separate these communities, and yet ships and camels
(the *ship* of the desert) make it possible to approach one another
across these unowned regions, and the right to the *earth's surface* that
belongs in common to the totality of men makes commerce possible.
The inhospitableness that coastal dwellers (e.g., on the Barbary Coast)
show by robbing ships in neighboring seas and by making slaves of
stranded seafarers, or of desert dwellers (the Arabic Bedouins), who
regard their proximity to nomadic peoples as giving them a right to
plunder, is contrary to natural right, even though the latter extends the
right to hospitality, i.e., the privilege of aliens to enter, only sofar as
makes attempts at commerce with native inhabitants possible. In this
way distant parts of the world can establish with one another peaceful
relations that will eventually become matters of public law, and the
human race can gradually be brought closer and closer to a cosmopolitan constitution. [14]

*It would not be inappropriate at the end of a war concluded by peace for a people to
set aside, after a festival of thanksgiving, a day of atonement so that in the name of the
nation they might ask heaven to forgive them for the great sin that the human race con-
tinues to be guilty of by failing to establish a lawful contract in relation to other peoples,
preferring instead, through pride in their independence, to employ the barbarous means
of war (by use of which they cannot secure what they seek, namely, the rights of each
particular nation). The festivals of thanksgiving for victories during war, the hymns
that are sung (in good Israelitic fashion) to the *Lord of Lords,* could not stand in greater
contrast with the idea of a Father of men, for besides displaying an indifference to the
way in which peoples seek their mutual right (which is sad enough), they actually express joy at having destroyed numerous humans and their happiness.

Compare this with the inhospitable conduct of civilized nations in our part of the world, especially commercial ones: the injustice that they display towards foreign lands and peoples (which is the same as *conquering* them), is terrifying. When discovered, America, the lands occupied by the blacks, the Spice Islands, the Cape, etc., were regarded as lands belonging to no one because their inhabitants were counted for nothing. Foreign soldiers were imported into East India under the pretext of merely establishing economic relations, and with them came subjection of the natives, incitement of various nations to 359 widespread wars among themselves, famine, rebellion, treachery, and the entire litany of evils that can afflict the human race.

China* and Japan (*Nippon*), which have had experience with such guests, have therefore wisely restricted contact with them. China only permits contact with a single European people, the Dutch, whom they nonetheless exclude as if they were prisoners from associating with the natives. The worst (or, considered from the perspective of a moral judge, the best) consequence of all this is that such violence profits these trading companies not at all and that all of them are at the point of near collapse. The Sugar Islands, the seat of the cruellest and most ingenious slavery, yield no true profit, but serve only the indirect and not very profitable purpose of training sailors for ships of war, which in turn aids the pursuit of wars in Europe. And this is the action of powers who, while imbibing injustice like water, make much of their piety and who in matters of orthodoxy want to be regarded as the elect.

Because a (narrower or wider) community widely prevails among 360 the Earth's peoples, a transgression of rights in *one* place in the world is felt *everywhere;* consequently, the idea of cosmopolitan right is not fantastic and exaggerated, but rather an amendment to the unwritten code of national and international rights, necessary to the public rights of men in general. Only such amendment allows us to flatter ourselves with the thought that we are making continual progress towards perpetual peace.

*[For the reasons why] we should call this great kingdom by the name it gives itself (namely, China, not Sina, or anything similar), one has only to consult Georgi's *Alpha* [*betum*] *Tibet* [*anum*], pp. 651-654, especially note b. According to the observation of Professor Fischer of Petersburg, there is actually no determinate name that it uses in reference to itself. The most common one is the word *"Kin,"* namely, gold (which the Tibetans call *"Ser"*), and therefore the emperor is called the king of *Gold* (i.e., of the most magnificent country in the world). In the kingdom itself, this word is probably pronounced *"Chen,"* but is pronounced *"Kin"* by the Italian missionaries (who cannot make the guttural sound). From this one can see that the Roman's so-called "Land of Seres" was China, and silk was brought from there to Europe across *Greater-Tibet* (probably through *Lesser Tibet,* Bukhara, Persia and so on). This leads to many speculations concerning the antiquity of this amazing nation in comparison with that of Hindustan, as well as regarding its connections with Tibet and also with Japan. But the name Sina or Tshina, which neighbors of this land give it, leads nowhere. Perhaps this also allows us to clarify the very ancient but never properly understood commerce of Europe with Tibet from what *Hysichius* has recorded about the hierophant's cry "Κονξ Ομπαξ" (*Konx Ompax*) in the Eleusinian mysteries. (See *Travels of the Young Anacharsis,* Part V, p. 447f.) For according to Georgi's *Alph. Tibet.* the word *"Con-* 360

First Supplement
On the Guarantee of Perpetual Peace

Perpetual peace is *insured* (guaranteed) by nothing less than that great artist *nature (natura daedala rerum)*,[16] whose mechanical process makes her purposiveness [*Zweckmassigkeit*][17] visibly manifest, permitting harmony to emerge among men through their discord, even against their wills. If we regard this design as a compulsion resulting

361   from one of her causes whose laws of operation are unknown to us, we call it *fate,* while, if we reflect on nature's purposiveness in the flow of world events, and regard it to be the underlying wisdom of a higher cause that directs the human race toward its objective goal and

362   predetermines the world's course, we call it *providence.** We cannot actually have *cognitive* knowledge of these intricate designs in nature, nor can we *infer* their actual existence from it, but (as with all relations between the forms of things and purposes in general) we can and must *attribute* them to objects only in thought [*hinzudenken*] so as to conceive of their possibility on an analogy with mankind's productive activities [*Kunsthandlungen*]. The relationship of objects to and their conformity with the purposes that reason itself sets out for us (the end of morality) can be represented from a *theoretical* point of view as a transcendent idea [*Idee*], but from the practical point of view (where, e.g., it is employed in relation to our concept of duty regarding *perpetual peace*), it is represented as a dogmatic idea and it is here that its reality is properly established. When, as in the context of this essay, our concern is entirely theoretical (and not religious) it is most appropriate to the limits of human reason to use the term *nature* (for in reflecting on the relations of effects to their causes, human reason must remain within the bounds of possible experience); the term

---

coia" means *God,* which has a striking resemblance to Konx. *Pah-cio* (*ibid.,* p. 520), which the Greeks might well have pronounced *pax,* means the *promulgator legis,* the divinity that pervades all of nature (also called *Cencresi,* p. 177). However, *Om,* which La Croze translated *benedictus, blessed,* can be related to divinity, but probably means nothing other than the *beatified,* p. 507. Now Fr. Franz Horatius often asked the Tibetan Lamas what they understood God (*Concioa*) to be and always received this answer, "It is the gathering of all the Saints" (i.e., the gathering of all blessed ones who, according to the Lama's doctrine of rebirth, have finally returned, after many migrations through all sorts of bodies, to the divinity, or *Burchane,* i.e., souls metamorphosed into being that is worthy of worship, p. 233). Thus that mysterious term *Konx Ompax* might well refer to that *holy* (*Konx*), *blessed* (*Om*) and *wise* (*Pax*) supreme Being who pervades the world (nature personified), and its use in the Greek *Mystery religions* may have signified a monotheism to the Epopts that contrasted with the polytheism of the people, though Fr. Horatius (among others) detected an *atheism* in it. But just how that mysterious term made its way from Tibet to Greece may apparently be explained in the foregoing way, as well as Europe's early commerce with China (which may have begun earlier than with Hindustan) through Tibet.[15]

*There is manifest in the mechanism of nature to which man (as a sensory being) belongs a form that is fundamental to its existence, a form that we cannot conceive except insofar as it underlies the purpose of a predetermining creator of the world. We call this predetermination (divine) *providence* in general; so far as it is established at the

nature is less *pretentious* than a term connoting that there is a *providence* of which we can have cognitive knowledge, and on which we take flight as on Icarus's wings in order more closely to approach the secrets of some unfathomable intention.

Before we define this guarantee [of perpetual peace] more closely, we must examine the state in which nature has placed her actors on her vast stage, a state that ultimately and necessarily secures their peace— then we shall see how she guarantees the latter.

363

Nature's provisional arrangement consists of the following: 1. She has taken care that men can live in all regions of the world. 2. Through *war* she has driven them everywhere, even into the most inhospitable regions in order to populate them. 3. Also through war she has constrained them to establish more or less legal relationships. It is truly wonderful that moss grows even in the cold wastes by the Arctic Ocean and that *reindeer* can dig it from beneath the snow so that they can become food or transportation for the Ostiak or Samoyed; or that the salt deserts are inhabited by the *camel*, which appears to have been created for traveling over them, so that the deserts do not go unused. But purpose is even more clearly evident when one realizes that not only do furbearing animals exist on the shores of the Arctic Ocean, but also seals, walruses, and whales, whose flesh provides food and whose blubber, provides warmth for the inhabitants. However, what most arouses our wonder is nature's care to bring (in what way we do not really know) driftwood to these barren regions, for without this material the natives could have neither their canoes and spears nor their huts to dwell in. In these regions they are sufficiently occupied with their war against animals that they live in peace among themselves.[22] But it was probably nothing but war that *drove* them there.

---

beginning of the world, we call it *grounding providence* (*providentia conditrix; semel iussit, semper parent,* Augustine);[18] where this purposiveness in nature's course is maintained through universal laws, we call it *ruling providence* (*providentia gubernatrix*); where it leads to specific ends [*Zwecken*] that men cannot foresee but can only infer from its results, we call it *guiding providence* (*providentia directrix*); finally, where we regard particular events as divine ends [*Zwecke*], we no longer speak of providence but of *dispensation* (*directio extraordinaria*). However, it is a foolish presumption for men to want to be able to recognize these latter for what they are (for in fact they are miracles, even though the events are not described in that way). No matter how pious and humble such language may be, it is absurd and altogether self-conceited to make an inference from some single event to some special principle as its efficient cause (so that this event is [regarded as] an end and not merely the natural and mechanical consequence of some other end completely unknown to us). In the same way, applying the distinction between *universal* and *special* providence (considered *materially*) to *objects* in the world is unjustifiable and self-contradictory (as when, for example, one claims that nature is concerned to preserve the species, but leaves individuals to chance); for the point of saying that providence applies universally is that no single thing is taken into consideration. Presumably, one intends by this to distinguish between the ways in which providence (considered *formally*) carries out its intentions, that is, in ordinary [fashion] (e.g., the annual death and revival of nature in accordance with the change of seasons) or in *extraordinary* fashion (e.g., the transport of wood by ocean currents to icebound coasts, where it cannot grow, so as to provide for the needs of their natives,

Among all the animals, the *horse* was the first that man learned to tame and to domesticate in the process of populating the earth and the first *instrument of war* (for the elephant belongs to a later period, to the luxury of already established nations). The art of cultivating certain kinds of grasses, called *grains,* whose original characteristics are no longer known, as well as the propagation and refinement of various *fruits* by transplanting and grafting (in Europe perhaps only two species, the crab apple and the wild pear), could arise only under conditions provided by already established nations, where property was secure; and it could occur only after men had already undergone the transition from the lawless freedom of hunting,* fishing, and herding

364   to the life of *agriculture. Salt* and *iron* were discovered next, and these were probably the first articles of trade sought far and wide by different peoples. In this way they entered into *peaceful relations* with one another, and from this common understanding, community of interest and peaceful relations arose with the most distant peoples.

In taking care that men *could* live everywhere on earth, nature has also despotically chosen that they *should* live everywhere, even against their inclinations, and without presupposing that this should rest on a concept of duty that binds men as a moral law; instead, she has chosen

---

who could not live without it). Here, while we can readily explain the physical and mechanical causes of these appearances to ourselves (e.g., by the fact that the banks of rivers in temperate lands are heavily wooded so that trees fall into them and are carried off by the Gulf Stream), we must nonetheless not overlook teleological causes, which indicate the care of a wisdom that governs nature. Only the scholastic concept of a divine *participation* in or concurrence (*concursus*) with every effect experienced in the world of sense must be given up. *First,* that scholastic view attempts to conjoin dissimilar kinds of things (*gryphes iungere equis*),[19] and it is self-contradictory to let that which is itself

362   the wholly sufficient cause of all changes in the world supplement its own predetermining providence in the course of the world (implying that providence must originally have therefore been lacking). It is, for example, self-contradictory to say that *after God,* the physician assisted in curing the illness. For *causa solitaria non iuvat.*[20] God creates the physician and all his medicines, and if we want to go back to the highest, but theoretically inconceivable,[21] original cause we must ascribe the action entirely to Him. Of course, if we explain this event as following from the chain of causes in the world and in accordance with the natural order, one can ascribe healing to the physician alone. *Second,* with that scholastic way of thinking we give up all determinant principles for making judgments about an effect. But from a *morally-practical* perspective (which is wholly directed to the supersensuous)—e.g., in the belief that if only our interactions are pure, God will compensate for our own injustices by means that are inconceivable to us and that we should not, therefore, give up our striving to do good—the concept of a divine *concursus* is entirely appropriate and even necessary. But it is self-evident that one must not attempt to *explain* a good action (as an event in the world) in this way, for that is a vain and consequently absurd attempt at theoretical knowledge of the supersensuous.

*Of all forms of life, the *life of the hunter* is without doubt most contrary to a civil-
364   ized constitution, for, having to live separately, families soon become estranged and, dispersed as they become in immense forests, also soon become enemies, for each requires a great deal of room in order to provide for its nourishment and clothing. The Noachic prohibition against blood (Gen. 9:4–5) (is repeated often, and Jewish Christians imposed it on pagans newly converted to Christianty as a condition of their acceptance, though for different reasons, Acts 15:20, 21:25) appears originally to have been nothing other than a command against the *hunting life,* since the latter often required eating raw flesh, and when the latter is forbidden, the other must also be.

war as the means whereby this purpose is to be fulfilled. Specifically, we see peoples whose unity of language reveals the unity of their origins, for instance, the *Samoyeds* of the Arctic Ocean, on the one hand, and a people with a similar language living two hundred miles distant, in the Altai Mountains, on the other; between them lives another people, of Mongolian origin, who are adept at horsemanship and, consequently, war and who drove the two parts of the other race into inhospitable arctic regions, where they would certainly not have gone of their own inclination.* Similarly, in the northern-most regions of Europe, Gothic and Sarmitic peoples, who pushed their way in, separated the *Finns,* called *Lapps,* by an equal distance from the linguistically related *Hungarians.* And what else but war—which nature uses as a means to populate the entire earth—could have driven the Eskimos (who are perhaps very ancient European adventurers, and totally distinct as a race from all Americans) to the north, and the Pescherais to the south of America, to Tierra del Fuego. Nonetheless, war itself requires no particular motivation, but appears to be ingrained in human nature and is even valued as something noble; indeed, the desire for glory inspires men to it, even independently of selfish motives. Consequently, *courage in war* (among American Indians as well as during Europe's chivalric period) is judged to be of immediate and great worth not only *during war* (as is reasonable), but also in order that *war might be,* and often war is begun only as a means to display courage. As a result, an intrinsic worth is bestowed on war, even to the extent that philosophers, unmindful of that Greek saying, "War is a bad bet because it produces more evil people than it eliminates," have praised it as having a certain ennobling influence on mankind. So much for what nature does to further *her own ends* in respect to the human race as a class of animal.

Our concern now is the most important question regarding the objective [*Absicht*] of perpetual peace: How does nature further this purpose that man's own reason sets out as a duty for him, i.e., how does she foster his *moral objective,* and how has it been guaranteed that what man ought to do through the laws of freedom, but does not, he shall, notwithstanding his freedom, do through nature's constraint? This question arises with respect to all three aspects of public right, *civil, international, and cosmopolitan right.* When I say of nature that she *wills* that this or that happen, that does not mean that she sets it out as a duty that we do it (because only practical reason, which is free of constraint, can do that); rather, she does it herself, whether or not we will it (*fata volentem ducunt, nolentem trahunt*).[23]

---

*One could ask, if nature has chosen that these icy coasts should not remain uninhabited and if (as we can expect) nature no longer provides them with driftwood, what will become of their inhabitants? For one must believe that as culture progresses, the natives in the temperate zone might make better use of the wood that grows on the banks of their rivers if they did not allow it to fall into rivers and float away into the sea. I answer: Those who dwell along the Ob, the Yenisei, the Lena, etc., will provide it through trade, exchanging it for products from the animal kingdom, in which the sea along the Arctic coasts abounds—but only if she (nature) first compels them to peace.

1. Even if a people were not constrained by internal discord to submit to public laws, war would make them do it, for according to the natural arrangement explained above, every people finds itself neighbor to another people that threatens it, and it must form itself into a *nation* so as to be able to prepare itself to meet this threat with *military might*. Now the republican constitution is the only one wholly compatible with the rights of men, but it is also the most difficult to establish and still harder to maintain, so much so that many contend that a republic must be a nation of *angels,* for men's self-seeking inclinations make them incapable of adhering to so sublime a form of government. But now nature comes to the aid of that revered but practically impotent general will, which is grounded in reason. Indeed, this aid comes directly from those self-seeking inclinations, and it is merely by organizing the nation well (which is certainly within man's capacities) that they are able to direct their power against one another, and one inclination is able to check or cancel the destructive tendencies of the others. The result for reason is the same as if neither sets of opposing inclinations existed, and so man, even though he is not morally good, is forced to be a good citizen. As hard as it may sound, the problem of organizing a nation is solvable even for a people comprised of devils (if only they possess understanding). The problem can be stated in this way: "So order and organize a group of rational beings who require universal laws for their preservation—though each is secretly inclined to exempt himself from such laws—that, while their private attitudes conflict, these nonetheless so cancel one another that these beings behave publicly just as if they had no evil attitudes." This kind of problem must be *solvable*. For it does not require the moral improvement of man; it requires only that we know how to apply the mechanism of nature to men so as to organize the conflict of hostile attitudes present in a people in such a way that they must compel one another to submit to coercive laws and thus to enter into a state of peace, where laws have power. One can see that although the inner core [crux] of morality is certainly not its cause, presently existing but still very imperfectly organized nations have in their foreign relations already approached what the idea of right prescribes (so that a good national consitution cannot be expected to arise from morality, but, rather, quite the opposite, a people's good moral condition [*Bildung*] is to be expected only under a good constitution). Consequently, the mechanism of nature, in which self-seeking inclinations naturally counteract one another in their external relations, can be used by reason as a means to prepare the way for its own end, the rule of right, as well as to promote and secure the nation's internal and external peace. This means that nature irresistibly *wills* that right should finally triumph. What one neglects to do will ultimately occur of its own accord, though with a great deal of inconvenience. "If one bends the reed too much, it breaks; and whoever wills too much, wills nothing."[24]

2. The idea of international right presupposes the existence of many *separate,* independent, adjoining nations; and although such a situa-

tion is in itself a state of war (assuming that a federative union among them does not prevent the outbreak of hostilities), yet this situation is rationally preferable to their being overrun by a superior power that melds them into a universal monarchy. For laws invariably lose their impact with the expansion of their domain of governance, and after it has uprooted the soul of good a soulless despotism finally degenerates into anarchy. Nonetheless, the desire of every nation (or its ruler) is to establish an enduring peace, hoping, if possible, to dominate the entire world. But nature *wills* otherwise. She uses two means to prevent peoples from intermingling and to separate them, differences in *language* and *religion*,* which do indeed dispose men to mutual hatred and to pretexts for war. But the growth of culture and men's gradual progress toward greater agreement regarding their principles lead to mutual understanding and peace. Unlike that peace that despotism (in the graveyard of freedom) brings about by vitiating all powers, this one is produced and secured by an equilibrium of the liveliest competing powers.

3. Just as nature wisely separates peoples that the will of every nation, based on principles of international right, would gladly unite through cunning or force, so also by virtue of their mutual interest does nature unite peoples against violence and war, for the concept of cosmopolitan right does not protect them from it. The *spirit of trade* cannot coexist with war, and sooner or later this spirit dominates every people. For among all those powers (or means) that belong to a nation, financial power may be the most reliable in forcing nations to pursue the noble cause of peace (though not from moral motives); and wherever in the world war threatens to break out, they will try to head it off through mediation, just as if they were permanently leagued for this purpose. By the very nature of things, large alliances for [purposes of waging] war are very rare and are even more rarely successful. In this fashion nature guarantees perpetual peace by virtue of the mechanism of man's inclinations themselves; to be sure, it does not do so with a certainty sufficient to *prophesy* it from a theoretical point of view, but we can do so from a practical one, which makes it our duty to work toward bringing about this goal (which is not a chimerical one).

Second Supplement
Secret Article for Perpetual Peace

Objectively, i.e., in the terms of its content, a secret article in pro-

*Differences in religion: an odd expression! Just as if one spoke of different *moralities.* No doubt there can be different kinds of historical *faiths,* though these do not pertain to religion, but only to the history of the means used to promote it, and these are the province of learned investigation; the same holds of different religious *books* (*Zendavesta,* the *Vedas, Koran,* and so on). But there is only a single *religion,* valid for all men in all times. Those [faiths and books] can thus be nothing more than the accidental vehicles of religion and can only thereby be different in different times and places.

ceedings concerning public right is a contradiction; but subjectively, i.e., judged from the perspective of the kind of person who dictates it, an article can certainly contain a secret [provision], for a person may find it beneath his dignity to declare openly that he is its author.

The sole article of this kind is contained in this sentence: *The maxims of philosophers concerning the conditions under which public peace is possible shall be consulted by nations armed for war.*

369
While it seems humiliating for the legislative authority of a nation, to whom we must naturally ascribe the greatest wisdom, to seek instruction from *subjects* (the philosophers) concerning the principles on which it should act toward other nations, yet it is very advisable to do so. Thus, the nation will *silently* (that is secretly) *seek their advice,* which is to say, it will *allow* them *to speak* freely and publicly about the universal maxims concerning the conduct of war and the search for peace (for they do it of their own accord already, if only one does not forbid it).[25] And an arrangement concerning this issue among nations does not require a special agreement, since it is already present as an obligation in universal (morally legislative) human reason. This does not, however, mean that the nation must give the principles of the philosophers precedence over the decisions of the jurist (the representatives of national power), but only that they be *heard*. The jurist, who has adopted as his symbol not only the *scales* of right but also the *sword* of justice, normally uses the latter not merely to keep the alien influences away from the former, but, when one side of the scales will not sink, to throw the sword into it (*vae victis*).[26] Every jurist who is not at the same time a philosopher (even in morality), is severely tempted by this practice; but his only function is to apply existing laws and to investigate whether they require improvement, even though, because his function is invested with power (as are the other two), he regards it as the higher one, when, in fact, it is the lower. The philosophical faculty[27] occupies a very low position in the face of the combined power of the other two. Thus it is said, for example, that philosophy is the *handmaid* of theology (and this is said of the two others was well). But one does not rightly know "whether this handmaid carries the torch before her gracious lady or bears her train behind her."

That kings should be philosophers, or philosophers kings is neither to be expected nor to be desired, for the possession of power inevitably corrupts reason's free judgment. However, that kings or sovereign peoples (who rule themselves by laws of equality) should not allow the class of philosophers to disappear or to be silent, but should permit them to speak publicly is indispensable to the enlightenment of their affairs. And because this class is by nature incapable of sedition and of forming cliques, it cannot be suspected of being the formulator of *propaganda*.

Preservation of freedom
Progress Culture
          (eg art &
(Gradual   science) Appendix   370

inter. Law for conduct btwn states

Amicable   On the Disagreement between Morals and Politics
  Union of   in Relation to Perpetual Peace
         Nations- cooperate + engage in mutual   Under-
                                                      stand-
    Taken objectively, morality is in itself practical, for it is the totality   voluntary
of unconditionally binding laws according to which we *ought* to act,
and once one has acknowledged the authority of its concept of duty, it
would be utterly absurd to continue wanting to say that one *cannot* do
his duty. For if that were so, then this concept would disappear from
morality (*ultra posse nemo obligatur*);[28] consequently, there can be no
conflict between politics as an applied doctrine of right and morals as
a theoretical doctrine of right (thus no conflict between practice and
theory). [If such a conflict were to occur], one would have to understand morality as a universal *doctrine of prudence,* i.e., a theory of
maxims by which to choose the most efficient means of furthering
one's own interests, which is to deny that morality exists at all.
    Politics says, *"Be ye wise as serpents,"* to which morality adds *(as a
limiting condition), "and innocent as doves."*[29] Where both of these
maxims cannot coexist in a command, there one finds an actual conflict between politics and morality; but if the two are completely
united the concept of opposition is absurd, and the question as to how
the conflict is to be resolved cannot even be posed as a problem. However, the proposition, *"Honesty is the best policy,"* is beyond all re-
futation, and is the indispensable condition of all policy. The divinity
who protects the boundaries of morality does not yield to Jupiter (the
protector of power), for the latter is still subject to fate. That is,
reason is not yet sufficiently enlightened that it can survey the series of
predetermining causes and predict with certainty what the happy or
unhappy consequences that follow in accord with nature's mechanism
from men's activities will be (though one can hope that they come out
as one wishes). But with respect to everything we have to do in order
to remain on the path of duty (according to rules of wisdom), reason
does provide us with enlightenment sufficient to pursue our ultimate
goals.
    Now even if the practical man [*Praktiker*] (for whom morality is   371
mere theory) admits that we can do what we ought to do, he bases his
disconsolate rejection of our fond hope on the following consideration: he asserts that, human nature being what it is, we can predict
that man will never want to do what is required to achieve the goal
[*Zweck*] of perpetual peace. Certainly, the will of all *individual* men
(the *distributive* unity of the wills of *all*) to live under a lawful constitution that accords with principles of freedom is not sufficient to attain this goal; only the will of *all together* (the *collective* unity of combined wills) is. The solution to so difficult a task requires that civil

society become a whole. Implementing this state of right (in practice) can begin only with *force,* and this coercion will subsequently provide a basis for public right, because an additional unifying cause must be superimposed on the differences among each person's particular desires in order to transform them into a common will—and this is something no single person can do. Furthermore, in actual experience we can certainly anticipate great deviations from that (theoretical) idea of right (for we can hardly expect the legislator to have such moral sensibilities that having united the wild mass into a people, he will then allow them to create a legal constitution through their general will).

For this reason it is said that he who once has power in hand will not have laws prescribed to him by the people. And once a nation is no longer subject to external laws it will not allow itself to be subjected to the judgment of other nations regarding the way in which it should seek to uphold its rights against them. Even a continent that feels itself to be superior to another, regardless of whether or not the latter stands in the way of the former, will not fail to exercise the means of increasing its power, plundering and conquering. Thus, all theoretical plans for civil, international, and cosmopolitan rights dissolve into empty, impractical ideals; by contrast, a practice that is based on empirical principles of human nature and that does not regard it demeaning to formulate its maxims in accord with the way of the world can alone hope to find a secure foundation for its structure of political prudence.

372   To be sure, if neither freedom nor the moral law that is based on it exist, and if everything that happens or can happen is mere mechanism of nature, then politics (as the art of using that mechanism to govern men) would be the whole of practical wisdom, and the concept of right would be a contentless thought. But if we find it absolutely necessary to couple politics with the concept of right, and even to make the latter a limiting condition of politics, the compatibility of the two must be conceded. I can actually think of a *moral politician,* i.e., one who so interprets the principles of political prudence that they can be coherent with morality, but I cannot think of a *political moralist,* i.e., one who forges a morality to suit the statesman's advantage.

The moral politician will make it a principle that once a fault that could not have been anticipated is found in a nation's constitution or in its relations with other nations, it becomes a duty, particularly for the rulers of nations, to consider how it can be corrected as soon as possible and in such a way as to conform with natural right, which stands in our eyes as a model presented by an idea of reason; and this ought to be done even at the cost of self-sacrifice. Since it is contrary to all political prudence consistent with morality to sever a bond of political or cosmopolitan union before a better constitution is prepared to put in its place, it would also be truly absurd that such a fault be immediately and violently repaired. However, it can be required of those in power that they at least take to heart the maxim that such changes are necessary so as continuously to approach the goal (of the constitution most in accord with laws of right). A nation may already possess republican rule, even if under its present constitution it has a despotic *ruling power,* until gradually the people are capable of being influenced by the mere idea of the law's authority (just as if it possessed physical power) and thus is found able to be its own legislator (which [ability] is originally based on [natural] right). If—through a violent *revolution* caused by a bad constitution—a constitution conforming to law were introduced by illegal means, it must not be permissible to lead the people back to the old one, even though everyone 373 who violently or covertly participated in the revolution would rightly have been subject to the punishment due rebels. But as to the external relations among nations, it cannot be expected that a nation will give up its constitution, even if despotic (which is the stronger in relation to foreign enemies), so long as it risks the danger of being overrun by other nations; consequently, it is permissible to delay the intention to implement improvements until a better opportunity arises.*

It may be that despotic moralists (those who fail in practice) violate rules of political prudence in many ways (by adopting or proposing premature measures); still, experience will gradually bring them to give up their opposition to nature and to follow a better course. By contrast with this, the moralizing politician attempts, on the pretext that human nature is not *capable* of attaining the good as prescribed in the idea of reason, to extenuate political principles that are contrary to right, and thus these principles make progress *impossible* and perpetuate the violation of right.

Instead of employing the practical science [*Praxis*] that these politically prudent [*staatskluge*] men make so much of, they use devious *practices* [*Praktiken*] to influence the current ruling power (so as to insure their own private advantage), even at the expense of the people and, where possible, the entire world, acting just like lawyers (for whom law is a *trade,* not a matter of *legislation*) when they go into politics. For since it is not their business to be overly concerned with legislation, but rather to carry out momentary commands under the law of the land, they must always regard every existing legal constitution as best—and when it is amended in higher places, they regard these amendments as for the best, too; in that way, everything follows 374

---

*These are permissive laws of reason: to allow a condition of public right afflicted with injustice to continue until everything is either of itself or through peaceful means ripe for a complete transformation, for any *legal* constitution, even if it conforms with right only to a small degree, is better than none, and the latter fate (anarchy) would result from *premature* reform. Political wisdom, therefore, will make it a duty, given the present state of things, to evaluate reforms against the ideal of public right. Revolutions brought about by nature itself will not find excuses for still greater oppression, but will use revolution as a call of nature to create a lawful constitution based on principles of freedom, for only this fundamental reform is enduring.

in its proper mechanical order. But, granted that this deftness at being all things to all men gives the politically prudent the illusion of being able to judge a *national constitution* in general against concepts of right (consequently, *a priori,* not empirically); and granted that they make a great to do of knowing *men* (which is certainly to be expected, since they deal with so many of them), though without knowing *man* and what can be made of him (for which a high standpoint of anthropological observation is required); nonetheless, if, as reason prescribes, they attempt to use these concepts in civil and international law, they cannot make the transition except in a spirit of charlatanism. For they will continue to follow their customary procedure (of mechanically applying despotically imposed laws of coercion) in an area where the concepts of reason only permit lawful compulsion that accords with principles of freedom, and it is under such principles alone that a rightful and enduring constitution is possible. The supposed practical man [*Praktiker*] believes he can ignore the idea of right and solve this problem empirically, the solution being based on his experience of the national constitutions that have heretofore been most lasting, though oftentimes contrary to right. The maxims that he uses to this end (though he does not make them public) consist, roughly speaking, of the following sophistries.

1. *Fac et excusa.*[30] Seize every favorable opportunity for arbitrary usurpation (of a right of a nation either over its own people or over another neighboring people); the justification can be presented far more easily and elegantly *after the fact,* and the violence more easily glossed over (especially in the first case, where the supreme internal power is also the legislative authority, which one must obey without argument), than if one first thinks out convincing reasons and waits for objections to them. This audacity itself gives a certain appearance of an inner conviction that the act is right, and after the fact the god of success, *bonus eventus,* is the best advocate.

2. *Si fecisti, nega.*[31] Whatever crime you have committed—e.g., that you have reduced your people to despair and hence brought them to rebellion—deny that the guilt is *yours;* instead, maintain that it is the obstinacy of the subjects, or, if you have conquered a neighboring people, that the guilt belongs to human nature, for if one does not forestall others by using force, one can surely count on their anticipating it and becoming one's conqueror.

3. *Divide et impera.*[32] That is, if there are certain privileged persons among your people who have merely chosen you to be their leader (*primus inter pares*),[33] destroy their unity and separate them from the people; and if, in turn, the people have delusions of greater freedom, everyone will depend on your unchecked will. Or if you are concerned with foreign nations, then sowing discord among them is a relatively certain method of subjecting them one after another to your will, all the while appearing to defend the weaker.

Certainly no one will be taken in by these political maxims, for all[6]

375

of them are widely known; nor are men ashamed of them, as if their injustice were altogether too apparent. For great powers never heed the judgment of the masses, feeling shame only in the face of others like them; and as regards the foregoing principles, not their becoming public knowledge, but only their *failure* can make those powers feel ashamed (for among themselves they agree on the morality of the maxims). And in this way their *political* honor, on which they can always count, is retained, namely, by the expansion of their power by whatever means they choose.*

*   *

*

From all these twistings and turnings of an immoral doctrine of prudence regarding how men are to be brought out of the warlike state of nature into the state of peace, we receive at least this much illumination: Men can no more escape the concept of right in their 376 private relations than in their public ones; nor can they openly risk basing their politics on the handiwork of prudence alone, and, consequently, they cannot altogether refuse obedience to the concept of public right (which is particularly important in the case of international right). Instead, they give this concept all due honor, even if they also invent a hundred excuses and evasions to avoid observing it in practice, attributing to cunning force the authority that is the original source and bond of right. In order to end this sophistry (if not the injustice that it glosses over) and to force the false representatives of those in earthly power to confess that rather than right it is might that they advocate—a fact that is clear from the tone they adopt, as if they

*Although we might doubt the existence of a certain inherent wickedness in *men* who live together within a nation, and instead might plausibly point to the lack of a sufficiently advanced culture (barbarism) as the cause of the unlawful aspects of their way of thinking [*Denkungsart*], this wickedness is still completely and incontrovertibly apparent in foreign relations among *nations*. Within each nation this wickedness is concealed by the coercive power of civil law, for the citizen's inclination toward violence against one another is counteracted by a greater power, namely, that of the government. Not only does this provide a veneer of morality (*causae non causae*), but by placing these inclinations toward outbreaks of lawlessness behind bars, it also actually makes it easier to develop the moral capacity for direct and immediate respect for the law. 376 Everyone believes of himself that he would truly venerate and abide by the concept of right, if only he could expect the same from everyone else, which it is government's part to insure; and by this means a large step towards morality is taken (although it is still not a moral step)—a large step towards willing the concept of duty for its own sake, without regard for any reciprocity. But since all persons have a good opinion of themselves but presuppose evil intentions in everyone else, they mutually have this opinion of one another, that they are all, in point of *fact,* of little worth (though how this might be remains inexplicable, since it cannot be blamed on the *nature* of man as a free being). Since, however, respect for the concept of right, which no man is capable of denying, provides the most solemn sanction for the theory that man has the ability to act according to it, everyone sees that for his own part he must act in accord with it, no matter how others may act.

were entitled to give orders—it will do well to expose the fraud to
which they subject themselves and others and to reveal the highest
principle from which perpetual peace as an end proceeds. We will
show that all the evil that stands in the way of perpetual peace derives
from the fact that the political moralist begins where the moral politician rightly stops; and, since the former subordinates his principles to
his ends (i.e., puts the cart before the horse), he defeats his own purpose of effecting an agreement between politics and morals.

377   In order to bring practical philosophy into harmony with itself, it is
first necessary to resolve this question: In problems of practical
reason, must we begin from *material principles,* the end [*Zweck*] (as
object of the will [*Willkür*]), or from its *formal* one, i.e., the one
(which rests only on freedom in external relations) that is expressed
thus: "Act so that you can will that your maxim ought to become a
universal law (no matter what the end [*Zweck*] may be)"?

Without doubt the latter principle must take precedence, because as
a principle of right it has unconditioned necessity, whereas the former
is necessary only if one assumes the existence of those empirical conditions through which the proposed end can be realized. And if this end
(e.g., perpetual peace) were also a duty, it must itself be derived from
the formal principle of external action. Now the first principle, that of
the *political moralists* (concerning the problem of civil, international
and cosmopolitan right), proposes a mere *technical task* (*problema
technicum*); by contrast, the second is the principle of the *moral politician,* for whom it is a *moral task* (*problema morale*), and its method
of pursuing perpetual peace—which one now desires not merely as a
physical good, but also as a condition that arises from acknowledging
one's duty—is completely distinct.

Solving the first problem, namely, the problem that political
prudence proposes, requires considerable natural knowledge so that
one can use nature's mechanism to attain the desired end; yet it is
uncertain how this mechanism will function as far as its consequences
for perpetual peace are concerned; and this is so in all three areas of
public right. Whether the people's obedience and prosperity will be
better preserved over a long period of time by harshness or by appeals
to vanity, by granting supreme power to a single ruler or to several
united ones, or, perhaps, merely by a devoted aristocracy or by the
power of the people is uncertain. History furnishes examples of the
opposite effects being produced by all forms of government (with the
singular exception of true republicanism, which alone can appeal to
the sensibility of a moral politician). Still more uncertainty arises in
the area of *international right*—a form of right purportedly based on
statutes worked out by ministers—for in fact it is a term without content, and it rests on contracts whose very act of conclusion contains
the secret reservation for their violation. By contrast, the solution to
the second problem, the problem of *political wisdom,* impresses itself
378 on us, as it were, for it obviously puts all artificiality to shame, and

leads directly to the end [*Zweck*]. Yet prudence cautions us not to employ power in direct pursuit of it, but rather to approach it indirectly through those conditions presented by favorable circumstances.

Thus, it may be said: "Seek first the kingdom of pure practical reason and its *righteousness,* and your end [*Zweck*] (the blessing of perpetual peace) will come to you of itself."[34] For this characteristic is inherent in morals—especially as regards its fundamental principle of public right (consequently, in relation to a politics that is *a priori* knowable)—that the less it makes conduct depend on the proposed end, be it a physical or moral advantage, the more conduct will in general harmonize with morality. And this is because such conduct derives directly from the general will that is given *a priori* (in a single people or in the relations of different peoples to one another), which alone determines what is right among men. If only it is acted on in a consistent way, this unity of the will of all can, along with the mechanism of nature, be the cause of the desired result and can make the concept of right effective. So, for example, it is a fundmental principle of moral politics that in uniting itself into a nation a people ought to subscribe to freedom and equality as the sole constituents of its concept of right, and this is not a principle of prudence, but is founded on duty. By contrast, political moralists do not even deserve a hearing, no matter how much they argue that the natural mechanism of a group of people who enter into society invalidates that fundamental principle and vitiates its intention, or seek to substantiate their contentions by use of ancient and modern examples of badly organized constitutions (e.g., of democracies without systems of representation). This is especially so since such a damaging theory may bring about the evil that it prophesies, for in it man is thrown into the same class as other living machines, which need only to become conscious that they are not free in order to become in their own eyes the most wretched of all the earth's creatures.

The true, albeit somewhat boastful proverb, *Fiat iustia, pereat mundus*—"Let justice reign, even if all the rogues in the world should perish"—is a sound principle of right that cuts across the sinuous paths of deceit and power. But it must not be misunderstood nor, perhaps, taken as permission simply to press with the utmost vigour for one's own right (for that would conflict with moral duty); instead, those in power should understand it to pose an obligation not to deny or diminish anyone's rights through either dislike or sympathy. Above all, this requires that the nation have an internal constitution founded on principles of right and that it also unite itself (analogously to a universal nation) with other neighboring and distant nations so they can settle their differences legally. This proposition means only that adherence to political maxims must not be based on the benefit or happiness that each nation anticipates from so doing—thus, not on the end [*Zweck*] that each nation makes an object (of its desire) and its supreme (though empirical) principle of political wisdom; instead,

379

adherence must derive from the pure concept of the duty of right
(from the *ought,* whose principle is given *a priori* through pure
reason), let the physical consequences be what they may. The world
will certainly not cease to exist if there are fewer bad men. The intrinsic characteristic of moral evil is that its aims (especially in relation
to other like-minded persons) are self-contradictory and self-destructive, and it thus makes way for the (moral) principle of goodness, even
if progress in doing so is slow.

*   *

*

Objectively (i.e., in theory) there is utterly no conflict between
morality and politics. But subjectively (in the self-seeking inclinations
of men, which, because they are not based on maxims of reason, must
not be called the [sphere of] practice [*Praxis*]) this conflict will always
remain, as well it should; for it serves as the whetstone of virtue,
whose true courage (according to the principle, *"tu ne cede malis, sed
contra audentior ito"*)[35] in the present case consists not so much in
resolutely standing up to the evils and sacrifices that must be taken on;
rather, it consists in detecting, squarely facing, and conquering the
deceit of the evil principle in ourselves, which is the more dangerously
devious and treacherous because it excuses all our transgressions with
an appeal to human nature's frailty.

380   In fact, the political moralist can say that the ruler and the people,
or the people and the people, do not treat *one another* wrong [*unrecht*]
if, through violence and fraud they war against one another, although
they do in general act wrong [*unrecht*] when they deny respect to the
concept of right, on which alone peace can be perpetually based.
When one person violates the rights of another who is just as lawlessly
disposed towards him, then whatever *happens* to them as they destroy
themselves is entirely right; enough of their race will always survive so
that this game will not cease, even into the remotest age, and they can
serve as a warning to later generations. In this manner, the course of
world events justifies providence. For the moral principle in man
never dies out, and with the continuous progress of culture, reason,
which is able pragmatically to apply the ideas of right in accordance
with the moral principle, grows through its persistence in doing so,
and guilt for transgressions grows concomitantly. (Given that the
human race never can and never will be in a better condition) it seems
impossible to be able to use a theodicy to provide any justification
whatsoever for creation, namely, that such a race of generally corrupt
beings should have been put on earth. We will be unavoidably driven
to such skeptical conclusions, if we do not assume that pure principles
of right have objective reality, i.e., that they permit themselves to be
applied and that peoples in nations and even nations in their relations
with one another must for their parts behave in conformity with them,

no matter how objectionable empirical politics may find them. Thus, true politics cannot progress without paying homage to morality; and although politics by itself is a difficult art, its union with morality is not art at all, for this union cuts through the [Gordian] knot that politics cannot solve when politics and morality come into conflict. The rights of men must be held sacred, however great the cost of sacrifice may be to those in power. Here one cannot go halfway, cooking up hybrid, pragmatically-conditioned rights (which are somewhere between the right and the expedient); instead, all politics must bend its knee before morality, and by so doing it can hope to reach, though but gradually, the stage where it will shine in light perpetual.

II   381

On the Agreement between Politics and Morality
under the Transcendental Concept of Public Right

If, in thinking about public right as jurists customarily do, I abstract from its *matter* (i.e., the different empirically given relations among men in a nation or among nations), the *form of publicity* [*Form der Publizität*], whose possibility every claim of right intrinsically contains, still remains, and unless every such claim has this form there can be no justice [*Gerechtigkeit*] (that can be regarded as *publicly knowable*), thus no right either, since the right can be conferred only through justice. Every claim of right must have this capacity for publicity, and since one can easily judge whether or not it is present in a particular case, i.e., whether or not publicity is compatible with the agent's principles, it provides us with a readily applicable criterion that is found *a priori* in reason; for the purported claim's (*praetensio iuris*) falseness (contrariness to right) is immediately recognized by an experiment of pure reason.

Having abstracted in this way from everything empirical contained in the concept of national and international right (such as the wickedness in human nature that makes coercion necessary), one can call the following proposition the *transcendental formula* of public right:

> "All actions that affect the rights of other men are wrong if their maxim is not consistent with publicity."

This principle is to be considered not only *ethical* (as belonging to the doctrine of virtue), but also *juridical* (as pertaining to the rights of men). If my maxim cannot be *openly divulged* without at the same time defeating my own intention, i.e., must be kept *secret* for it to succeed, or if I cannot *publicly acknowledge* it without thereby inevitably arousing everyone's opposition to my plan, then this necessary and universal, and thus *a priori* foreseeable, opposition of all to me could not have come from anything other than the injustice with which it

threatens everyone. Further, it is merely *negative,* i.e., it serves only as
382 a means for recognizing what is *not right* in regard to others. Like any
axiom, it is seen in the following examples of public right.

1. In regard to *civil right* (*ius civitas*), namely, rights internal to a
nation, the following question arises, one that many believe is difficult
to answer, but that the transcendental principle of publicity solves
with utter ease: "May a people rightfully use rebellion to overthrow
the oppressive power of a so-called tyrant (*nontitulo, sed exercitio
talis*)?" The rights of the people are injured, and no injustice comes to
him (the tyrant) who is deposed, of that there is no doubt. Nonetheless, it remains wrong in the highest degree for the subjects to pursue
their rights in this way, and they can in no way complain of injustice if
they are defeated in this conflict and must subsequently suffer the
harshest punishment for it.

A great many arguments can be offered on both sides when one attempts to settle this issue by a dogmatic deduction of the foundations
of right. Only the transcendental principle of the publicity of public
right will spare us this long-windedness. According to this principle,
before establishing the social contract, the people have to ask whether
it dare make known the maxim of its intention to revolt in some circumstances. One can readily see, first, that if one were to make revolt
a condition of the establishment of a nation's constitution that force
might then in certain circumstances be used against the ruler and, second, that the people must in such an instance claim some rightful
power over the ruler. In that case, he would not be the ruler; or if as a
condition of establishing the nation, both the people and the ruler
were given power, there would be no possibility whatsoever of doing
what it was the people's intention to do. The wrongness of revolt
revealed by the fact that the maxim through which one *publicly
declares it* renders one's own intention impossible. One must therefore
necessarily keep it secret. This secrecy, however, is not necessary on
the part of the nation's ruler. He can say quite openly that he will
punish with death the ringleader of every rebellion, even if they believe
that he has been the first to transgress the fundamental law. For if he
knows that he possesses *irresistibly* supreme power (which must be
assumed in every civil constitution, since he who lacks sufficient might
383 to protect each of his people against every other, also does not have
the right to give orders), he does not have to worry that his own intention will be defeated if his maxim becomes known. It is perfectly consistent with this view that if the people's revolt succeeds, the ruler,
returning to the status of a subject, cannot begin a new revolt to return
himself to power, nor should he have to fear being called to account
for his previous administration of the nation.

2. *Concerning international right:* There can be talk of international right only on the assumption that a state of law-governedness
exists (i.e., that external condition under which a right can actually be
accorded man). For as a public right, its concept already contains the

public recognition of a general will that determines the rights of everyone, and this *status iuridicus* must proceed from some contract that cannot be founded on coercive laws (like those from which the nation springs), but can at best be an *enduring free* association, like the federation of different nations mentioned above. For in the state of nature, in the absence of a state of law-governedness, only private right can exist. Here another conflict between politics and morality (considering the latter as a doctrine of right) arises, to which, however, the criterion of the publicity of maxims finds easy application, though only if the contract binds the nations for the sole purpose of maintaining peace among themselves and between them and other nations, and not with the intention of conquest. This introduces the following instances of antinomy between politics and morality, along with their solution.

(a) "If one of these nations has promised something to another, be it aid, cession of certain territories, or subsidies, and so on, it may be asked whether, in those cases where the nation's well-being is at stake, it can be released from its promise by maintaining that it must be considered to have two roles: first, that of a sovereign, who is answerable to no one in the nation; and, on the other hand, merely that of the highest *political official,* who must give an account of his actions to the nation. From this we draw the following conclusion, that what the nation has bound itself to by virtue of its first role, it frees itself from in its second." But if a nation (or its ruler) were to allow its maxim to be known, then all the others would quite naturally either flee from it 384 or would unite with others in order to oppose its arrogance. This proves that, given all its cunning, politics would in this way (through openness) defeat its end [*Zweck*]; consequently, that maxim is wrong.

(b) "If a neighboring power grows so formidably great (*potentia tremenda*) as to cause anxiety, can one assume that it will want to oppress others because it *can;* and does this give the lesser powers a right to (unified) attack on it, even without previous injury?" A nation that *let it be known* that it affirmed this maxim would suffer evil even more certainly and quickly. For the greater power would beat the lesser ones to the punch, and, as far as concerns the union of the latter, that would only be a feeble reed against one who knew how to employ the maxim *divide et impera.*

(c) "If a smaller nation is so located that it divides some territory that a larger one regards as necessary to its preservation, is not the latter justified in subjugating the smaller one and incorporating it into itself?" One can easily see that the larger must not allow it to become known that it has adopted such a maxim; for either the smaller nations would unite very early, or other powers would fight over the prey, and, consequently, openness would render the maxim ineffectual, a sign that it is wrong, and, indeed, perhaps to a very high degree. For a small object of wrong [action] does not prevent the wrong done to it from being very great.

3. Here I silently pass over the issue of *cosmopolitan right,* for, given its analogy with international right, its maxims are easy to adduce and validate.

*   *

*

In the principle of the incompatibility between the maxims of international right and publicity one has a good indication of the *incommensurability* of politics and morality (as a doctrine of right). But one now needs also to become aware of the conditions under which the maxims of politics agree with the right of peoples. For it cannot be

385   conversely concluded that whatever maxims are compatible with publicity are also for that reason right, for he who has decisively supreme power, has no need to keep his maxims secret. The condition underlying the possibility of international right in general is that there first exist a *state of right* [*rechtlicher Zustand*]. For without this there is no public right, and all right other than this (in the state of nature) that one can think of is merely private right. Now we have seen above that a federative state [*föderative Zustand*] of nations whose only purpose is to prevent war is the only state of *right* compatible with their *freedom.* Thus, it is possible to make politics commensurable with morality only in a federative union (which is therefore necessary and given *a priori* in conformity with the principles of right); and the foundation of right underlying all political prudence is the establishment of this union to the greatest possible extent, for without this as an end all the sophistry of political prudence is contrary to wisdom, hence mere veiled wrong. The *casuistry* of this pseudopolitics is unsurpassed by the best of the Jesuit scholars, including as it does the *reservatio mentalis,* i.e., formulating public contracts in such terms (e.g. the distinction between a *status quo* of *fact* and of *right*) that, whatever the occasion, one can interpret them in one's own favor; including, further, the *probabilismus,* i.e., attributing evil intentions to others, or making the likelihood of their possible superior power into a justification of the right to undercut other, peaceful nations; and, finally, the *peccatum philosophicum* (*peccatillum, baggatelle*), i.e., maintaining it to be an easily dismissible triviality to devour a *small* nation when some purportedly very much *greater* benefit to the world is the result.*

Politics' duplicitous relation to morality by first using one of its branches and then the other in pursuit of its purposes is fed by this casuistry. Both the love of man and the respect for the rights of man

*Documentation for such maxims can be found in Counselor Garve's treatise *"Über die Verbindung der Moral mit der Politik,"* [*On the Unity of Morality and Politics*], 1788.[36] This worthy scholar admits at the outset that he is unable to give an adequate answer to this question. But to approve of this union while granting that one cannot fully meet the objections that can be brought against it seems to be more forebearing than is advisable toward those who will most tend to misuse it.

are our duty; the former is only *conditional,* while the latter is a *un-conditional,* absolutely imperative duty, a duty that one must be completely certain of not having transgressed, if one is to be able to enjoy the sweet sense of having done right. Politics readily agrees with   386 morality in the first sense (as ethics) for both surrender men's rights to their rulers. But with regard to morality in the second sense (as doctrine of right), before which it must bend the knee, politics finds it advisable not to enter into any relation whatsoever and, unfortunately, denies all reality to morality and reduces all duties to mere benevolence [*Wohlwollen*]. This ruse of a secretive politics could be easily defeated were philosophy to give publicity to the maxims of politics, if politicians would only allow philosophers to give publicity to their own.

With this in mind, I propose another transcendental and affirmative principle of public right, whose formula is:

> "All maxims that *require* publicity (in order not to fail of their end) agree with both politics and morality."

For if they can achieve their end only through publicity, they must also conform to the universal public end (happiness), and it is the singular task of politics to establish this (to make the public satisfied with its state [*Zustand*]). But if this end can be attained only by publicity, i.e., by removing all mistrust of the maxims through which it is to be achieved, these maxims must harmonize with public right, for in this latter alone is the unity of all ends possible. I must postpone the further development and explanation of this principle for another occasion. But that it is a transcendental formula can be seen from the absence of all empirical conditions (of the doctrine of happiness), as material of the law, and from the reference it makes to the mere form of universal lawfulness.

If it is a duty to make the state of public right actual, though only through an unending process of approximation to it, and if at the same time there is a well founded hope that we can do it, then *perpetual peace,* which will follow the hitherto falsely so-called treaties of peace (but which are really only suspension of war), is no empty idea, but a task that, gradually completed, steadily approaches its goal (since the times during which equal progress occurs will, we hope, become ever shorter).

Notes for
Perpetual Peace

References to essays in this volume are to page numbers in the *margins*.

1. A. A., VIII, 341–386. *Perpetual Peace* was first published in 1795 in Königsberg by Friedrich Nicolovius; a second, enlarged edition appeared in 1796. The specific occasion for which Kant wrote the essay is unknown, but speculation is that he was moved to do so by the signing of the Treaty of Basel on April 5, 1795.

2. See *Theory and Practice*, note 14, p. 92–3.

3. See *Theory and Practice*, 298, 303 and *Perpetual Peace*, 384–86.

4. See *Theory and Practice*, 290–96.

5. See *Universal History*, 26.

6. Reichsgraf Joseph Niklas Windisch-Graetz (1744–1802), proposed a prize question regarding the formulation of contracts in such a way that they could have only a single interpretation, thereby eliminating disputes over the transfer of property.

7. Kant's conception of the state of nature is clearly similar to, perhaps influenced by, Hobbes's. Kant would have been able to read either Hobbes's *De Cive,* where the state of nature is discussed in chapter 1, section 12, or the Latin translation of Leviathan, where the relevant discussion is chapter 13, as it is in the original English version.

8. See Note on the Text, p. 26. See *Theory and Practice*, 290 ff.

9. Frederick II (The Great) of Prussia.

10. Jacques Mallet du Pan (1749–1800) in *Über die französische Revolution und die Ursachen ihrer Dauer* (1794) (*On the French Revolution and the Causes of its Duration*). du Pan was a Swiss born opponent of the revolution.

11. Alexander Pope, *Essay on Man* III, 303–4.

12. H. Grotius (1583–1645), *De jure belli et pacis,* 1625; Samuel von Pufendorf (1632–1694), *De jure naturae et gentium,* 1672; Emer de Vattel (1714–1767), *Le droit des gens,* 1758.

13. "And godless Furor shall sit/Inside on his frightful weapons, hands bound with a hundred/Brass knots behind him, and roar with

bloody mouth. Vergil, *Aeneid* I, 294–96. (Lind translation)

14. Many of the themes in this Article are also covered in *Spec. Beg. Human History*.

15. This arcane note reveals an important and charming aspect of Kant's personality, his utter fascination with all matters concerning the development of human culture.

16. "every need/pours from the lap of earth and magic nature." Lucretius, *The Nature of Things,* V, 233–4. (Copley translation)

17. The terms *Zweck* and *Zweckmässigkeit* have given all of Kant's translators problems. I have chosen "end" as my primary English translation of *Zweck,* though I do sometimes use "goal." Both connote the consequence or result that one intends to achieve by adopting a particular plan and pursuing a specific course of action, and these are at the heart of Kant's use of the term. For *Zweckmässigkeit,* however, I have chosen "purposiveness," which is a traditional rendering that, in fact, comes close to capturing Kant's sense. The only problem is that my choice of English equivalents for the German terms fails to preserve graphically the linguistic relationship among them. But I see no way of doing the latter and of maintaining good English sense, and the latter must ultimately take precedence.

18. "Providence conditions; once she commands, they always obey,"

19. "griffins may yet mate with mares." Vergil, *Eclogues,* VIII, 27. (Lewis translation)

20. A single cause suffices.

21. Here and in what follows Kant's discussion turns on his distinction between the dogmatically theoretical and the morally practical perspectives. The dogmatically theoretical perspective is the one from which we finite creatures can properly speak of having cognitive knowledge of things. Such knowledge involves *both* a sensory *and* a conceptual element. Without both, Kant argues in the *Critique of Pure Reason,* what we tend to think of as demonstrably true scientific knowledge is not possible. On the other hand, there are some matters of vital interest to creatures such as ourselves about which, though we can have no knowledge of the foregoing type, we must necessarily have beliefs. Specifically, we all do have beliefs about freedom, immortality and God, and these are matters that Kant argues we can consider only from the morally practical perspective. His view, then, is that we cannot have dogmatically theoretical knowledge of their existence and nature, but from the morally practical perspective we are justified in having beliefs about them. See

A 633/B 661 - A 636/B 664 and A 797/B 825 - A 819/B 847; see also *Crit. Judgment,* 179–186.

22. See *Spec. Beg. Human History,* 118 ff.

23. "The fates lead him who is willing, but drag him who is unwilling." Seneca, *Epist. mor.* XVIII. 4. See *Universal History,* 17, *Theory and Practice,* 310, and *End of All Things,* 337.

24. Friedrich Bouterwek, (1766–1828).

25. See *Enlightenment,* 40.

26. Woe to the vanquished.

27. Kant's reference here is to the organization of the German university of the time, which consisted of three "higher" (graduate) faculties of Theology, Law, and Medicine, and a "lower" (undergraduate) faculty of Philosophy. His view, expressed in *The Contest of the Faculties,* is that while the three "higher" faculties might properly be subject to control by the government, since they train persons to perform in areas of specific concern to the government, the "lower" faculty educates persons as persons, and should therefore be free of both government control and control by the "higher" faculties.

28. Beyond possibility there is no obligation.

29. Matt. 10:16; compare also Hume, *Enquiry Concerning Morals,* 271.

30. Act first, then justify.

31. If you are the perpetrator, deny it.

32. Divide and conquer.

33. First among equals.

34. Matt. 6:33.

35. "do not yield to misfortune, but press on more boldly/Than your fortune allows you." Vergil, *Aeneid,* VI, 95. (Lind translation)

36. Christian Garve (1742–1798), *Abhandlung über die Verbindung der Moral mit der Politik oder einige Betrachtungen über die Frage, inwiefern es mögliche sei, die Moral des Privatlebens bei der Regierung der Staaten zu beobachten* (Breslau, 1788). (*Treatise on the Connection of*

Morality with Politics, or Some Questions on the Extent to which It Is Possible for the Governments of Nations to Observe Morality in Private Lives.)

Glossary

Absicht intention, objective
äußere Freiheit external freedom
Anlage capacity

Befolgung compliance
Befugnis authority, privilege
Begier desire, appetite
Bestimmung vocation (of man); determination (of objects)

erkennen to know cognitively
Erkenntnis cognitive knowledge

Fähigkeit capacity
Feindseligkeit hostility
Fortgang progression

Gegenmacht opposing power
gemeins Wesen commonwealth
gemeinsamer Wille general will
Glaubenssatz articles of faith
Gutseigntumer landowner

Hang tendency

Idee idea

kunstlich contrived
Kunsthandlung inventive activity

Lust pleasure

Mitgesetzgeber co-legislator
Mituntertan co-subject
Motiv motive

Naturtrieb natural urge, instinct

Naturzustand state of nature
Neigung inclination, propensity

Obrigkeit government

Publizität publicity

Recht right
Rechtanspruch claim of right
Rechtslehre doctrine of right

Schicksal fate
Staat nation
Staatsklugheit political prudence
Staatsoberhaupt nation's ruler
Staatsrecht civil right
Staatsverwaltung nation's government

Trieb impulse
Triebfeder incentive
tugendhaft virtuous (person)
Tugendlehre doctrine of virtue

unrecht wrong, unjust
Untertan subject

Verderbnis corruption
Verfassung constitution
Verfügung decree
Vermögen ability
Vertrag contract
Volk people
Volksrecht international right
Vorrecht privilege
Vorsehung providence
Vorteil advantage, benefit

Weltbürger   citizen of the world,
cosmopolite
Willensbestimmung   determination
of the will

Zufriedenheit   contentment
Zustand   state

Index

38-39; as empirical, 39; and fiction, 49; of freedom, 49; governed by man, 11; governed by nature and providence, 11; as idea, 38; individual and species in, 11; as leading to a perfect constitution, 36; as leading to man's full development, 36; as man's transition from animality to humanity, 11; process of, 11; as realization of nature's hidden plan, 36; speculative, 49

History, universal: contributes to man's development, 38-39
Hobbes, Thomas, 82, 91
Horatius, Fr., 120n.
Human actions: as appearances, 29
Human history: as systematic, 29
Human nature: as physical and moral, 13; and social existence, 32
Hume, David, 4-5, 12, 15

Idea, 16-17; of reason, 77, 95
Ideals: development of, 52
Immaturity, 41, 73; intellectual and as being reliant on authority, 2; epistemological and metaphysical, 2; intellectual and moral, 2
Imperative, Categorical, 47, 68
Imperatives, 9; practical, 10
Inclinations, self-seeking: counteraction of, 124
Inequality: increase of among men, 57
Innocence: man's fall from, 54
Instinct, 31, 51; sexual, 51; as voice of God, 50

Japan, 119
Judgment, 61; day of, 93
Justice, public, 56; law of, 77

Kepler, Johannes, 30
Knowledge: cognitive, 104; synthetic a priori, 8, 16

Laborers: and artisans, 76n.
La Croze, Mathurin Veyssiere (de), 120n.
Land: ownership of, 57
Lao-Kiun (Lao Tze), 99
Law: civil, 112n.; coercive, 74, 89; duty to, 78; external, 72; freedom

under universal, 72; general, 111n.; and happiness, 78; as legislation, 129; moral, 64n., 66; moral as man's ultimate end, 64; permissive, 110, 111n., 129n.; prohibitive, 110, 111n.; public, 75, 77, 79; public coercive, 13, 72; publicity of, 44; resistance to, 79; respect for as the moral motive, 10; and right, 75; right of resistance to, 78; as trade, 129
Leaders: injustice of, 80
Legislation: and freedom, 102; supreme principle of, 83
Leibniz, Gottfried Wilhelm, 5
Lessing, Gotthold Ephraim, 85
Life: shortness of, 58
Locke, John, 1, 3
Lord, gracious, 75n.
Love: definition of, 101
Luxury, 57

Machines: men more than, 46
Man: as end in himself, 10, 53; first, 50; first beginnings of, 49; maxims of the practical, 130-31; as natural and moral species, 54; as nature's end, 52; needful of a master, 33; and other rational beings, 53; practical, 127
Marcus Aurelius, 115n.
Master: required for society, 33-34
Maxim: political, 130-1; as universal legislation, 65
Men: inequality among, 56n.
Mendelssohn, Moses, 85-86
Mentality: Christian, 102; patriotic, 73
Mercenaries, 108
Might: right and, 127
Monarchs: rights of, 82
Monarchy: hereditary, 108
Moralist: political, 128-30, 132-34
Morality, 127; and culture, 96; incentive of, 66; necessary for culture, 36; politics and, 138; politics and conflict between, 127, 134; and skepticism, 4
Morals: theory and practice in, 71
Motives: our knowledge of, 69; of the will, 67

Nations: constraints on, 115; external relations among, 34, 129; federa-